A RAIN OF WORDS

CARAF BOOKS

*Caribbean and African Literature
Translated from French*

Carrol F. Coates, EDITOR

Clarisse Zimra, J. Michael Dash,
John Conteh-Morgan,
& Elisabeth Mudimbe-Boyi,
ADVISORY EDITORS

A RAIN OF WORDS

A Bilingual Anthology of Women's Poetry in Francophone Africa

EDITED BY Irène Assiba d'Almeida

TRANSLATED BY Janis A. Mayes

University of Virginia Press

Charlottesville and London

University of Virginia Press
© 2009 by the Rector and Visitors of the University of Virginia
All rights reserved
Printed in the United States of America on acid-free paper

First published 2009

9 8 7 6 5 4 3 2 1

Library of Congress Cataloging-in-Publication Data

A rain of words : a bilingual anthology of women's poetry
in Francophone Africa / edited by Irène Assiba d'Almeida ;
translated by Janis A. Mayes.
    p.   cm. — (CARAF books)
Includes bibliographical references and index.
ISBN 978-0-8139-2765-7 (cloth : alk. paper) —
ISBN 978-0-8139-2766-4 (pbk. : alk. paper)
1. African poetry (French) — Women authors — Translations
into English.   2. African poetry (French) — Women
authors.   I. Almeida, Irène Assiba d'.   II. Mayes, Janis Alene.
PQ 3986.5.E5R35 2009
841'.9140809287 — dc22   2008038345

To the memory of Grace d'Almeida
My beloved sister
Who for me encompassed all that a woman should be:
Rich in spirit
Rich in family
Rich professionally
With tenacious drive
Having the plight of women at heart and
    aiming to pave the road to justice.
Knowing the joys of poetry, and holding it dear.
        IRÈNE ASSIBA D'ALMEIDA

In memory of my dad, Allen Mercer Mayes,
who loved the music and truth-telling of poetry,
and in honor of my mother, LaVerne Hadnott Mayes,
who loves the pictures of life in the written word.

        JANIS A. MAYES

Where to find the perfect word

Where to find the perfect word
For the door of silence
To open the dance of the story
Next to my woman's skin
That God created
As an instrument of unwritten music.

TANELLA BONI

Closed for Inventory

There is nothing to sell today
No smile
No sweet word
No sour word
No sweet and sour word
I am closed
Closed for inventory

I am not buying anything today
No crazy laugh
No sweet talk
No sour talk
No sweet and sour talk
I am closed
Closed for inventory

The entire store will be inspected today
The empty shelves
The full shelves
The half-empty shelves
The half-full shelves
Everything will be dusted
Everything will be checked
Everything will be rechecked
Everything will be counted
Everything will be weighed on a scale
Nothing will be ignored
On the left tray the assets
On the right tray the liabilities

Tomorrow if everything isn't up for grabs
If some energy is left for selling
If she finds her wholeness again
The store will open again, maybe
But today there is nothing for sale
Nothing to buy, nothing to grab
I am closed
Closed for inventory

MONIQUE ILBOUDO

CONTENTS

ACKNOWLEDGMENTS

I would like to thank the University of Arizona for supporting this project with several travel and research grants. I would also like to thank the Tanner Humanities Center at the University of Utah for awarding me an Eccles Research Fellowship in 1997–98. Special thanks must go to Cathie Brettschneider, the humanities editor at the University of Virginia Press, as well as Carrol Coates, the CARAF series editor, for extending their support to this work from the very beginning. Among my family and friends, I would like to particularly thank my daughter Senami d'Almeida for her loving support and Lee Van Demarr, who followed this anthology closely over the years and offered invaluable advice. To my graduate assistants, Corey Gagné, Yvonne Marie Mokan, Sylvester Mutunda, and Raymond Gnanwo Hounfodji, I offer my most sincere appreciation; the help they offered at different stages of the project was crucial to the end result. I certainly need to thank the many, many people in the countries of West and Central Africa, in France, and in Belgium who helped by pointing out relevant books and magazines or giving me names and introducing me to poets. This anthology could never have been completed without their knowledge and assistance. Special mention must be made here of Christiane Laïfaoui, who provided me with a list of poets that helpfully complemented my initial list. I also wish to credit Renée Larrier, whose early article on Senegalese women poets helped inspire me to pursue this project. Above all, I would like to thank the poets themselves for their many contributions to this book and most of all for the rain of words, beautifully and generously offered like a precious gift.

IRÈNE ASSIBA D'ALMEIDA

For reading and listening to various versions of *A Rain of Words,* I thank especially: Chelsea Lemon Fetzer and Andrée-Anne Kekeh; Carrol Coates and Carole Boyce Davies; Greg Thomas, Diana Biro, and my Uncle Billie, William H. Hadnott Jr.

For their continuous enthusiasm about this project, I thank my students.

For the research leave and funding awarded, I am grateful to Syracuse University and the College of Arts and Sciences.

JANIS A. MAYES

INTRODUCTION

Contemporary Griottes and Stubborn Town Criers: The Making of an Anthology

IRÈNE ASSIBA D'ALMEIDA

The Genesis

A Rain of Words [Une pluie de mots] is a bilingual anthology of poetry written by women in francophone Africa, the first comprehensive anthology of its kind. To me, this book is a celebration of francophone African women marking their place in the literary world, and in the larger world as well. My hope is that the texts here and the English translations provided by Janis Mayes, a friend in sisterhood, a colleague and collaborator in this project, will help make this work accessible to a wide range of readers who enjoy and love poetry, while simultaneously allowing for the voices of these women to be heard globally.

Perhaps the most important thing women poets have brought to African poetry is what seems most obvious: the woman's point of view. I believe, however, that this vantage point is the source of much of what is beautiful and valuable in this body of work. Our title, *A Rain of Words,* reflects the general belief, held by many African cultures, that "in the beginning there was Water, and Water was of God, and Water was God." In Fon, one of my native tongues, the word for woman is *"gnonnu,"* which means literally, "to know how to drink." In a land prone to disastrous droughts, water is precious and vital. Woman symbolically joined to water reminds us of her essential role in bringing and sustaining life. Beyond the culturally inscribed geo-poetic image it evokes, "a rain of words" also connotes a sense of uninterrupted abundance, which to me aptly describes women's production of poetic words.

To speak of poetry written by francophone African women is to speak significantly of today and tomorrow, but to speak very little of yesterday. My "yesterday" is not quite literal, of course, as it indicates that the history of poetry published by women in francophone Africa is a very short one. Indeed, the beginning of francophone African women's poetry can be assigned to a specific calendar year. In 1965, Annette Mbaye d'Erneville, a producer for Senegal's National Radio, published her book titled *Poèmes africains,* reprinted later as *Kaddu.* This was the first book of poetry in French published by an African woman, and it was so well received that it was awarded the Prix des poètes sénégalais de langue française. Despite that initial acclaim and its important founding role, d'Erneville's book has largely disappeared from any history of African or francophone literature.

A slow trickle of titles followed in the 1970s, and then a great many more books of poetry by francophone African women emerged in the decades after 1980—some from African publishing houses, others from publishers in France. The fact of publication has not, however, meant long-standing literary recognition for d'Erneville or her successors. Their books have rarely been reprinted, their poems rarely anthologized and even more rarely translated into other languages, and thus the poets have received very little critical attention. Even poets who manage to continue writing and publishing in this kind of vacuum seem to do so out of a personal need, or stubbornness, rather than from a sense of connection to a literary community within their country or region. This limbo for women poets that I observed in francophone Africa, and the "disappearance" of a body of work that I knew was both excellent and extensive, was what served as my inspiration for this project. The contradiction I faced—knowing African women were writing important poetry in French, yet rarely seeing it published or even mentioned—moved me to launch the anthology as a full-scale book.

The state of affairs for these talented poets was a condition I found unfathomable. One can only begin to understand them within the immediate contexts of African history. Marking the start of francophone African women's poetry in 1965 puts it at the center of a decade that was pivotal for the political history of the entire continent. In the twentieth century, that history, much simplified, can be divided into a "before" and an "after": the continent before independence and the continent after independence. Very roughly, for the first sixty years of the last century, Africa was a continent of colonies, and for the last forty years it became, to some degree, "free." That the publication of *Poèmes africains* and the struggles for the end of French colonial rule in Africa occurred together is not coincidental, though to say that does not mean there is a direct connection between the two events. I believe a history and the literature of the time are linked, but not in a simple way that is diagrammatic or necessarily apparent. So, while *Poèmes africains* is a book that celebrates a new nation's independence, which is a political and historical matter, the fact that its author was a woman is also a historical and political matter, in a less obvious way. If d'Erneville wrote at a moment of historic hopefulness, she also wrote as someone who was not supposed to be a writer, at least not of a book of poems. Her contradictory position is symptomatic of the complex circumstances of literature, politics, gender, and history at any given time.

The independent Africa that we live in and live with today is frequently described as "postcolonial." The word is problematic but also unfortunately accurate as a description, because the continent remains strongly marked by the colonial era—the residual effects ripple still. The three major colonial powers—France, Great Britain, and Portugal—began in the nineteenth century to conquer and divide Africa into their separate spheres of influence. Whether for political advantage or convenience, or even on a whim, they carried out a policy of further fragmentation within these spheres, which produced the political geography still represented on maps of contemporary Africa. The mystifying patchwork of those maps has little to do with autochthonous geographical formations, historical realities, or cultural traditions of the land and its people. Rather, it was the result of imposing arbitrary political forms on an underlying heterogeneity, which the colonizers were either indifferent to or did not understand. There is no doubt that Africa's current problems of ethnic conflict, class differentiation, and gender inequalities are to some extent the result of the geopolitical chaos left over from the colonial period. In 1965, however, most people in Africa did not foresee these future calamities. It was a time of exhilaration, of hope, and of expectation: a new beginning.

The end of direct colonial rule in West and Central Africa was closely associated with a literary movement that began in Paris in the 1930s among francophone students from Africa and the Caribbean. This movement would be called Negritude, and its blend of literature—particularly its poetry—and politics would have an enormous influence on all the African liberation movements that arose after World War II. Negritude became a movement for political independence, while always retaining its literary focus and a profound desire for the recognition of African cultures and civilizations. Its liberating discourse—especially its poetry—intended to celebrate and create an awareness of those cultures. The Negritude writers wanted to energize a strong collective political consciousness through that awareness, though they were writing in French rather than in any of their native African languages. The advantages of using French, both to deal with the West and as a common tongue among themselves, were obvious, and the argument of turning the ruler's weapons, in this case their very language, against the rulers, was attractive.

Negritude very successfully created a myth with which to resist the colonial myths of African inferiority—the ubiquitous racism that was used to
justify the *mission civilisatrice,* the economic exploitation, the political sub-
jugation. The new myth, however, while it accurately recovered African civi-
lization and exposed European hypocrisy, also imposed a belief in a cultural
coherence and the possibility of a "Pan-Africanism" that proved difficult to
achieve. The cultural ruptures engendered by colonization inevitably led to
the crises that have continued to plague the continent and that Negritude's
ideological idealism was not prepared to deal with effectively.

One of the problems with this idealism was its view of women. In its po-
etical practice Negritude offered an idealized picture of "woman" and de-
veloped a kind of formula of interchangeable relations in which woman =
mother = earth = Africa = Mother Africa. Any number of fine poems were
written expressing this formula and vision. Of course, in this vision most of
the reality of "woman's condition" was lost. At the same time the masculinist
and masculinocentric bias in Negritude discourse made it reluctant to recognize the important participation of women, who had helped in the prac-
tical and theoretical development of the movement, relegating their contributions to the secret history where women's work is all too often buried.[1]

However ironic, the limitations of these masculinist representations were
a major inspiration that propelled women into writing. It helped inspire
what I call a *"prise d'écriture"* or a "seizing of writing," in the sense of a militant appropriation of the written word and a strong determination to fash-
ion a *nouvelle écriture.* Despite this effort to "seize" writing, there was an in-
stitutional and cultural resistance, in Africa and in Europe, to seeing women
as poets. African women could write poems in French, publish them, be
read and known locally, and yet be ignored by the larger literary and critical
world. On a global scale, their work was unknown, ergo, ignored, to the loss
of all poetry readers, while their sense of presence within a community of
writers was severely diminished. Excluded from a wider African readership,
they would know each other's work only intermittently, and thus the body
of their work falls into what I call an "empty canon": unknown, unpraised,
uncriticized.

It is not surprising, therefore, that the poetry of this anthology is so little
known within literary institutions and has been unavailable to most readers
until now. I became increasingly aware of its absence as I tried to assemble
texts for classes in francophone African literature and found that the only
published writing by women was fiction. Indeed, when I looked into anthologies of African poetry for selections, I found that when they existed

they often included very few women or none at all. This seemed a strange situation since I knew female poets in francophone Africa had been writing almost a decade before any book of fiction by a woman appeared.[2]

The Making of an Anthology

I felt it was time to try and redress a stunning imbalance in African literature. It was necessary to intervene in the formation of an African literary canon and to demand that it recognize and include the poetry of women. It seemed necessary to go from the written word to the printed page, and the only way to manage this was to become a more activist scholar, like a "town crier" in the African tradition—a stubborn town crier going from publishing house to publishing house, offering a generous bag filled with women's poetic words: "a rain of words."

I soon realized that this project would have to begin almost from scratch as far as texts were concerned, and that I would have to spend considerable time and effort in the field. In the summer of 1993 I traveled to Togo, to Côte d'Ivoire, to Senegal, and to Benin, collecting books and magazines, contacting literary people, seeking out poets, asking for their work and for the names of other poets, and tape-recording interviews with them whenever possible. This work became my preoccupation, but still it had to be done between many other professional and personal responsibilities, and had to be supported by travel grants and seemingly never enough vacation time. As a result the research advanced at a slower pace than I had hoped for.

It was the summer of 1996 before I could investigate the archives in Paris and Brussels where a good deal of information about francophone Africa is cataloged. The final month of that summer I traveled to the Sahel, searching for poets in Burkina Faso, in Mali, and in Niger. My last trip was in 1998, when I visited Mauritania. My discoveries in these travels exceeded even my own expectations: the francophone women in Africa today have written an *enormous* amount of poetry. Much of it has been published by European presses, but a substantial part appeared from local African publishers, who are rarely distributed outside the continent and who often have a limited and local circulation within their town or country. There are also more poets and poems than there are publishers—I read excellent manuscripts which have yet to find a press, and I am certain that there is still much more outstanding work that I have not had the good fortune to see.

Of course this project became something I discussed frequently with colleagues, asking for advice and looking for ideas. A group I spoke with at an

African Studies Association meeting in 1995 convinced me the anthology should be bilingual—French and English—to make it accessible to more American readers and more English speakers in Africa and elsewhere, perhaps even more attractive to publishers as well. Janis Mayes then joined me in my endeavor. I collated and assembled the considerable collection of material, finally producing a rough version of what would be the finished anthology. The translation was still a major task before us, but we felt we should begin talking to publishers. The responses from these initial contacts, and my reflections on those responses and reactions, were invaluable. They made me fine-tune my thinking about what exactly I wanted this anthology to be and why, exactly, it had to be that way.

There was certainly interest in the project, but there were also serious reservations about the version of the book I described. First, they concerned the problem of the "empty canon." Publishers frequently asked me, "Who are these poets?" "What have been the criteria of your selections?" "Why are you including unknown, even unpublished poets?" The questions were not entirely illegitimate, since, in the Western canon, an anthology usually must be assembled along specific lines, as the etymology of the word suggests. In Greek, "antho" is "flower" and "logy" is "to collect." So "anthology" means "flower gathering," hence the word *florilège* in French. The implication here is that what is gathered must be as beautiful as a bouquet of flowers, a collection of the best pieces of a literary genre that have survived the test of time.

Publishers who have worked with this conception of an anthology would naturally challenge my selection criteria, which they saw as a deliberate nonselection. But what I wished to represent was, in part, the abundance, the variety, and the geographical reach of poetic activity among women in francophone Africa. I wanted to show not only individual flowers, but a flourishing. Of course my selections had to involve personal judgments about a poem's value, most often in the absence of any sanction by international presses or critical attention. A canon may appear to be empty not because there is nothing in it, but because no one has bothered to look inside. Finally, it is my belief that the argument that because a poet is unknown she therefore should not be published is a hopelessly circular one: how can she become known without being published?

My determination to be a "town crier" was reinforced by the resistance I received when seeking a publisher for this anthology. I felt a vital need to proclaim the value and necessity of such work. My resolve was further strengthened by the thought of how such critical engagement—the readers' reactions that I had received—was rare for the poets whose writing I had collected. An anthology could help seed a discussion and help create a critical context that had not existed before. It could help overcome an absence of attention from the critical world, which can only result in artistic death.

I was asked why I was not including male poets in the anthology. This question brought me abruptly back to my project's original starting point. Quite simply, my interest was not in excluding men. Rather, my goal was to devote, for the first time in history, full attention to the women poets who have been virtually invisible in African literature written in French. I wanted to assemble an anthology that would offer a collection of this largely unknown work; I wanted to spotlight women in particular as a way of suggesting that the canon needs to be revised, and even subverted. In the same way as the Negritude movement was imperative at a specific historical moment in order to establish a Black literary presence and a Black identity, I believe the publication of anthologies of female writers is a necessary, hopefully transitory, act imposed upon us by history itself. The existence of francophone African women as writers of poetry needs to be established as a fact.

It is a fact to me. This anthology was begun in 1993 and I continue to discover women poets from West and Central Africa, and new books of poetry from the region continue to appear every year. The forty-seven poets included in this anthology come from twelve countries in West and Central Africa. All but three of them are alive and working, primarily in Africa, but a few in Europe and in North America. If some worthy poets have not been included here, it is only because I came to know of their existence too late. Most of these women are, however, featured in the bibliography. I am certain that omissions still exist, but my hope is that this anthology will be followed by many more of its kind in the future.

I have resisted the temptation to classify the poets by country. Rather, I present them in alphabetical order, though I also indicate their country of origin. The reader thus has the choice of literary cartographies: reading the poems as coming from a specific geographical location or simply reading them as poems by African women. Words in African languages, Wolof from Senegal, Fon from Benin, for example, appear in some poems as do place-names such as Abidjan, Dakar, Ouagadougou. This deliberate identification explains, in part, why some critics speak of "national literatures" in Africa, though these contemporary nation-states are of course not indigenous, but remains of colonial configurations.

Reading the poems simply as poems by African women would be to take a Pan-African approach, especially taking into consideration the fact that a number of these poets were born in one African country, grew up in another, and now live in a third, within or outside the continent. Nationalities therefore are more fluid, and these writers can be seen as belonging to a Pan-African entity, thus foregrounding what Aminata Traoré calls the "Nous fédérateur" [the "federating Us"], the collective consciousness that accounts for cultural unity at a continental level.[3]

The Female Poet as Contemporary *Griotte*

I see the poets included in this anthology as contemporary *griottes* (*griotte d'aujourd'hui*),[4] because African women, in the oral as well as the written tradition, both as custodians of cultural lore and educators of children, have been the choice producers and composers of lyrics in various genres. At the same time, the term "griottes" is fraught with the contradictions of the past and the challenges of the present. Even though being a "griotte" is an important profession, it is also inscribed within a lower caste in the social hierarchy of several African societies. As a result, a number of poets included in this anthology being of noble origins told me that they did not wish to be associated with "griottes." Yet the title of this introduction is inspired by "Griot de ma race" [Griot of my race], a poem by the Senegalese writer Ndéye Coumba M'Bengue Diakhaté, who proudly proclaims: "I am the griot of my race." These two contrasting positions illustrate why the term "griotte" is used here. It shows that oscillating between the strength of traditional values and the tyranny of tradition, women are positioned at the very heart of the dialectics between continuity and change.

There is a further historically rooted conflict concealed here, one that I alluded to in discussing Negritude and which is implicit in the term "francophone." In March of 2007, a number of "francophone" writers based in Paris called into question the term and proposed that so-called "francophone" literature be renamed "La littérature-monde en Français" or "world literature in French."[5] I find this new term, a sort of bow to literary globalization, rather vague, however, and more importantly, it undercuts or even erases a critical political history. For all its shortcomings, the term "francophone" reminds us that the writing it designates arises from a specific political and historical context, a series of relations in time and space that involve ruler and ruled, *"métropole"* and "periphery," colonizers and colonized. The effects of that history will not disappear by supplying a new term of identification; more likely, they will only be hidden or disguised.

Therefore, despite the objections and the reservations that I had in the past to the idea and the very term of "francophonie," I feel today that we do not need a term such as "littérature-monde en Français." Rather, what we need is to understand "francophone" in a new way. Though francophone, this poetry is decidedly *African*. And it is in realizing its African nature and meaning that we may escape, or at least begin to neutralize, the historical entrapments that a term such as "francophone" still holds. Thus it becomes most important that the French language variously expressed by these women poets be understood in relation to all of the African contexts—both past and present—out of which their poetry emerges.

Francophone African women poets do not ostentatiously lament the fact that they use French as a medium for poetry. Yet women poets may view the French language as both a political and a patriarchal imposition, and linguistically as having formal and structural formations that make it more difficult to express their gendered experience. Diakhaté plays with the meaning of griot to evoke and apparently celebrate a tradition even as she questions it. She uses the masculine form of the word "griot" in her title, thus posing a problem from the onset: is the female poet speaking of herself, or is her reference to the usual male singer of stories and of history?

This situation shows that the woman poet finds herself in an untenable position of locution, forced as she is to use a patriarchal language, and at the same time to resist its patriarchal implications. It is only in this posture of tension that she will be able to write. In addition, she must free herself from traditional impositions that dictate for her a specific type of speech, clothed with the modesty that the society deems fitting for a woman. Having achieved linguistic freedom, the woman poet can now express herself in a manner free of constraints, without taboos. Her liberated pen can raise feminist themes to address patriarchy, but also can speak about sensuality and desire, about the woman's body no longer as a site of suffering but as a site of pleasure.

For all of its subtlety, African women's poetry is highly militant. It deliberately moves away from established paradigms even within the most universal, common themes. The great themes of human emotion are sung or cried over, exalted or cursed. Love—be it passionate, painful, or disappointing—is celebrated, as are friendship, happiness, pain, solitude, and the ultimate separation, death. These women poets have not avoided controversial topics, investing their poetry with social and political content. The liberated pen is biting and caustic in its denunciation of inequalities, the injustices of the shantytowns of contemporary cities or the historical wrongs represented by Gorée and Soweto. It is in the manner of modern griots that they sing the praises of liberation leaders like Lumumba, Sankara, and Um Nyobe, even as they decry the exploitative political regimes, the atrocities of war and genocide, the destructions of globalization, and the disruptions of immigration and exile.

If the mythical image of the mother is rejected, children still occupy a central place in the literary landscapes drawn by women. This fundamental preoccupation is a logical continuation of the new sociopolitical discourse formulated by women. Children obviously are the ones who suffer most from the failed political systems, and because children are the future of nations, through poetry, women take it upon themselves to teach new generations how to understand, resist, and subvert old categories of thinking. This teaching is at the same time rooted in, and valorizes, an African view of the world. This poetry may celebrate Africa as did the Negritude writers, while also presenting children with new paradigms pregnant with the seeds of a better future.

If the themes of this poetry are varied, they are most often expressed in simple, direct language that is aesthetically pleasing with its sound and rhythm, inspired by the African oral traditions where women have always played a pivotal role. The militant character of this melodious poetry does not rob the text of its aesthetic value. It is an aesthetic which is often grave— one of tension, of paradox, and of rupture. It also has its light tones, both oneiric and ludic, often bearing the mark of irony and even sarcasm. The language, at its best wonderfully innovative, reveals the magical character of words, resounding with rhythm, undulating with movement. It is also poetry of the future—an immense cloth on which women embroider with carefully chosen words their dreams of today, of years past, and of years to come. And so, in an elaborate ritual of words—at once evasion and meditation, challenge and compromise, incantation and vociferation, song and cry—the voice of these women poets resonates loudly, always beautifully, sometimes heartrendingly, but relentlessly creating multiple echoes that resist silence.

The ritual of words remains a primary means for people to understand, critique, and possibly make sense of the increasingly complex conditions of their lives, while creating the opportunity for linkages between people. I, as an editor of this book, am an African woman, born under a colonial regime, educated in Africa, Europe, and the United States, and am now a long-practicing academic within the Western system of professional scholarship. My situation is hardly unique today, in an era when colonialism has metamorphosed into diverse forms of globalization. Yet the poetry in this anthology restores my memory of a different lived history and an awareness of the complex sets of happenstance by which I have come from there to here. And here, I am a member of the new diaspora, meeting, across the Atlantic, the old diaspora through Janis Mayes, an African American woman, born into histories of slavery and segregation, educated in the United States,

Europe, and Africa, a scholar and translator. Together, we have engaged in a fruitful collaboration, bringing a new poetry from the Old World to the New. A trans/lation has taken place, in a sense much larger than just rendering a text into another language. In doing this work, we are renewing the diasporic connections that have always made for vital interchange among Black people located on all sides of the Atlantic, an "Atlantic of a Thousand Crossings."

Notes

I should mention that many of the authors I have included have written long poems, some of them notable book-length poems, in fact. In such cases, I have selected specific sections for translation. I have also made the editorial decision to silently emend typographical errors that appeared in the French texts.

1. This situation has finally begun to change. See T. Denean Sharpley-Whiting, *Negritude Women* (Minneapolis: University of Minnesota Press, 2002).
2. If, for historical reasons, crucial anthologies such as those edited by Leopold S. Senghor (1948) or Lilyan Kesteloot (1967) did not include women, such exclusion is no longer acceptable. However, it should be noted that beginning in the 1990s there have been more women poets included in the new anthologies. Among the best of these are *Poésie d'Afrique au Sud du Sahara,* edited by Bernard Magnier, and more recently Hamidou Dia's anthology, *Poètes d'Afrique et des Antilles* (2002), one of the most inclusive to date. There is still, however, a long road ahead before we see a fair representation of poetic production by African women.
3. Aminata D. Traoré. *L'étau: L'Afrique dans un monde sans frontières* (Paris: Actes Sud, 1999), 14.
4. In African oral traditions a griotte (the feminine form of griot) is defined as: a) a poet and often musician trained in the art of eloquence, b) an individual entrusted with the memorization, recitation, and teaching of oral history from one generation to the next, c) a professional singer of praise and criticism, a social commentator.
5. A book came out of this position. See Michel Le Bris and Jean Rouaud, eds., *Pour une littérature-monde* (Paris: Gallimard, 2007).

TRANSLATOR'S NOTE

Reverberations of African Culture and Women's Creativity in Poetry

JANIS A. MAYES

> You went into that forbidden territory and decolonized it and ungated it . . . so that in your wake we could enter it, occupy it, restructure it in order to accommodate our complicated passion—our intricate, difficult, demanding beauty, our tragic, insistent knowledge our lived reality, our sleek classical imagination—all the while refusing "to be defined by a language that has never been able to recognize [us]."
> —Toni Morrison, *Eulogy for James Baldwin, 1987*

African Life Beats from the Bottom of Her Words

A Rain of Words compiles the work of forty-seven African women poets from "francophone" territories. Many of the women are previously unpublished or published in important local or regional presses in Africa where neocolonial social conditions and political economies often preclude wide or regular publication and distribution to encourage their work. Some of the poets here have received wide international visibility. Together they expand the record of African and African Diasporan women's writing as they are authorized through the research of Irène Assiba d'Almeida, a leading scholar of African francophone women's literature, also a poet, colleague, and friend in sisterhood.[1] Approaching these texts as a literary translator, scholar, and teacher of African and Diasporan literatures in French and English translation, I expect this anthology to expand work in several fields, including Black studies and translation studies, as well as comparative literature and gender studies.

As individuals, these forty-seven women poets share a common writing language. As part of a larger collective of multilingual poets from the African world, they can be read in French and in English via TransAtlantic (or, sAlt) translation: a practice and theory of translation that I have conceptualized and named. Formulated during the process of translating *A Rain of*

Words and of analyzing fiction by Toni Morrison in French translation, sAlt translation assesses and seeks to resolve questions of language politics, culture, and literacy involved in translating authors from Africa and the African Diaspora.[2] I focus especially on women writers who refuse to be defined by languages and translation practices and theories that have never been able to recognize them as artists or locate their particular creative expression. In *A Rain of Words,* everyday experiences and life-threads pulled from fabrics of African material cultures are filtered through the women's imagination and woven into aural literature.

In an earlier essay[3] I provide a new definition of the word to "translate," which is revisited here to illustrate my approach to translating *A Rain of Words.* This definition derives from an understanding of translation as a lived reality and experience located in irrevocable history. The term "translation" is embodied; the word to "translate" is freighted. Twelfth-century-French and fifteenth-century-English etymologies of the word "translate" derive from the Latin *transferre,* which means to transfer, move, or carry over from one place to another, and by extension to transform, turn one language into another.[4] The word takes on original meaning when African women, men, and children are brought from Africa as human cargo in slave ships, moving in many directions across Atlantic Ocean waters, through the Middle Passage, into new "homes," new identities, new and reappropriated languages and ways of knowing and being Black. The passages over water were not silent. People translated the experience and lived reality across water into what I call Middle Passage Language,[5] and into new art forms and artistic inventions. It is from this irrevocable history of translation that "francophone" emerges as a word and concept in relation to colonization, an outgrowth of slavery. In *A Rain of Words,* Kouméalo Anaté is translated to say,

> Words like swords
> Words of stone
> Words like bullets
> Cut into the flesh
> From naked feelings blood
> Flows in a torrent
> Today
> Tomorrow
> Yesterday
> Maybe forever?

Reverberations

All translation begins with questions. I am using this key word and musical term "reverberations" to mean the rhythmic movement of sound heard as echoes of ideas; reflection of light and deep-sightedness as seen in meta-phors and images; memory and heat, pulsating from dynamic sources, over and again. "Reverberations" is a concise response to a multidimensional and open-ended question. How can one explore the poetics and functioning of the poems that constitute *A Rain of Words (Une pluie de mots)* without privi-leging either of the languages used? In what directions is the poetry mov-ing? Where are the derivatives and possibilities of this poetry by African women poets from "francophone" African territories located?

The term "francophone" has a troubling history. France, of course, par-ticipated in slavery on a massive scale, followed by a colonizing apparatus that included French language as an ideology, a tool of assimilation, within French-occupied territories. "To call a person Francophone," d'Almeida writes, "veils the fact that the person does have another language . . . an Af-rican language."[6] Layered with social and political dynamics, "francophone" is generally understood to mean "French-speaking" or where French is spo-ken. My use of the term involves the actual Greek word behind the "-phone" in "franco-phone," φωνή, which means sound, tone, "properly, the sound of the voice."[7] Tracing the term back to the ear, to the sound of the voice, I in-terpret "francophone" to mean "where French is heard."

Further, the francophone question continues to invite compelling public scholarship and literary response.[8] In *A Rain of Words,* some poets amplify specific African languages—Fon, Pulaar, and Wolof—not as artifacts but as living languages. In other examples, drum language functions as a trope for requisite knowledge and fluency called for in today's world. One can also identify poets who occupy French language in ways for which it was never intended, claiming ownership and freedom of expression within and across dominating frameworks.

In translating the poems of *A Rain of Words,* I take the stance of a jazz vocalist or instrumentalist, with a clear sense of the historical, cultural, and political activity surrounding the poem. First, I look for the idea as though seeking the tone note and image. Next, I explore and analyze rhythmic pat-terns in relation to ideas, coded messages, gestures, and sounds reverber-ated on each line and throughout the poem. I see the French language and the English language as "voices over" the activity and meanings the poet conveys. The translation is not a copy of the poem, nor an exact equivalent; it is a vivid memory I evoke of the poem in my mind. The Atlantic Ocean was not and is not a silent space. African women in slave ships spoke African languages and translated sounds, words, and experiences into new art forms enriched by threads of memory. This understanding of translation as memory is a critical component of the TransAtlantic (sAlt) translation theory I have formulated. The close analysis, personal experience, and memory I bring to bear on each poem are akin to improvisation as articulated by the preeminent music critic Ralph Ellison, who puts it this way: "True jazz is an art of individual assertion within and against the group . . . each solo flight, or improvisation, represents a definition of his identity as individual, as member of the collectivity and as a link in the chain of tradition."[9]

I write the poem out, play it out aurally and in my head, then test it with a keen listener—Irène. We exchange notes. We change places. Repetition. I listen for the music and newness in the language. I search for logic and meanings in the flow of words and sounds. Repetition. Yes. Translation is never truly over. In the African contexts I return to, African languages thrive, not at intersections of French, but often as dominant languages in the public sphere functioning in the same geopolitical environment. One hears a creolization of French with cadence and rhythmic patterns that disturb French language status quo. Also, there is status quo French that is occupied by African women's experience and imagination. There are African languages heard in the public sphere sprinkled with French. In classrooms and lecture halls one hears the French of the academy. African women poets from francophone territories are multilingual, and this is why *A Rain of Words* is polyphonic and polysemous.

A Rain of Words is a memory of *Une pluie de mots.* Therefore, the English translation is a new textual invention. You will hear and read a variety of French language articulations in the English version. I see translation functioning like a delayed memory of the past, or, in musical terms, a reverberation of sound and memory emanating from two (or more) speakers with a slight delay of one with respect to the other, creating an echo-like sound.[10] This slight delay can be a split second, or even reach back to the eighteenth century, which, for me, can be understood as a beginning, or point of departure, for the African women poets and their poetry, more precisely, of what is found, not lost, in translation.

As the literary translator of this and any work, I am visible, in tune with the ethics and engaged with the politics of translating into English this poetry in French by African women. Translation is not a neutral process. The language politics of the translator come into play. Translators have an agenda whether it is hidden or not. We make decisions. We know that what gets translated is what gets read, and in turn, is what we read and know. So we must ask ourselves, for whom is this new textual invention intended? To what uses can it be put to expand reading constituencies, to reinforce or dismantle reading patterns and hierarchies? What happens or is expected to happen as a consequence of the translation? How, in what specific ways, by what methods and strategies used, does the translator render the sound quality, cultural meaning, and language politics of the writer? Or does the translator write the author back into a language and status quo that were never intended to recognize, or authorize her? To whom does the translation belong?

In a way, this original poetry anthology, *A Rain of Words,* can be understood as a delayed response to, or reverberation of, the poetry and literary translation practice of an African woman from Wolof culture called Phyllis Wheatley (1753?–1784). In her poem *On Being Brought from Africa to America* (1773), and in her translation *The Negro Equalled by Few Europeans* from the French, *Le nègre comme il y a peu de blancs* (an antislavery novel by Joseph La Vallée), Wheatley asserts her identity and authority as an African woman writer.[11] She carries into her creative intellectual work memory that resonates with experience. Brought from the coast of Senegal at the age of seven or eight as cargo on a slave ship named *Philis,* then bought as property that carried the Wheatley name, her solo acts of poetry and translation worked within and against the group—within and against the master text, as Toni Morrison might put it. Phyllis Wheatley "ungates forbidden territory," creating space for African "francophone" women poets to thrive in translation.

Black Women on the Move

In the hands of readers, the poets of *A Rain of Words* take their rightful place beside other literary traditions that emerge from experiences of slavery, colonialism, migration, and domestic and foreign domination across dynamic, ongoing histories. As an entire work, *A Rain of Words* is relocated into old and new creative expressions. Lyrical book language can be read in conversation with percussive drum language. Allusions and references illuminate the work of African writers, intellectuals, filmmakers, and political figures throughout the Pan-African world. Art forms such as blues songs, folk tales, and the visual arts are evoked.

I have translated these poets into English not only for North American and British readerships but for all English speakers, readers, and listeners, especially in Africa and African Diasporas. The pathbreaking anthology edited by Carole Boyce Davies *Black Women's Writing* was instrumental in establishing the international dimensions of Black women's writing.[12] Further, I want to encourage literary translation analysis and discussion of strategies used by the translator. I hope to have inspired new intertextual readings, re-translations, and reimaginings of these poems across all artificial borders of land and water. Even more, I hope this book is simply enjoyed, talked about, shouted, and rapped about for generations to come.

Reverberating in my mind, a woman's lyrical voice says in Wolof, *nan ko bokk,* or, "Let's share it."

Notes

I borrow the expression "Life Beats from the Bottom of Words," in the first subheading, from MC Solo, a pioneer of hip-hop in France. Solo presented this anti-universalism idea in his discussion on a panel The Politics of Hip-Hop Culture in France, as part of Paris Noir: Literature, Art and Contemporary Life in Diaspora, a summer seminar (Syracuse University Abroad, Department of African American Studies), Paris, June 22, 2007. I am grateful to Paris Noir seminar students, guest artists, and the scholar Samir Meghelli for their fresh insights. See also Greg Thomas, "Pan-Africanism and Sexual Imperialism," in *The Sexual Demon of Colonial Power: Pan African Embodiment and Erotic Schemes of Empire* (Bloomington: University of Indiana Press, 2007), 1–23.

1. For an example of d'Almeida's scholarship, see *Francophone African Women Writers: Destroying the Emptiness of Silence* (Gainesville: University Press of Florida, 1994).

2. My formulation and naming of this concept, TransAtlantic literary translation, or sAlt translation, is part of a larger project in progress inspired by the translation practices of Mercer Cook. Drawing upon particular elements of cultural fluency, notably jazz aesthetics in his translation of scholarship by Cheikh Anta Diop, and "diaspora literacy" in his critique of English translations of Negritude poetry, Mercer Cook is an important literary translator, a forerunner in the field. See, for example, Brent Hayes Edwards, *The Practice of Diaspora: Literature, Translation, and the Rise of Black Internationalism* (Cambridge, Mass.: Harvard University Press, 2003).

3. In addition to a new definition of the term "translate," I introduce a new usage for the tilde (~) diacritic. For example, in Fatou Sow's "A Day at Gorée," the tilde refers to sound where there is language in French yet no words in the English translation. The tilde is therefore transformed into a beat that resonates from the source language into the target culture, and vice versa. See Janis A. Mayes, "'Her Turn, My Turn': Notes on TransAtlantic Translation of African Francophone Women's Poetry," in

"Femmes Africaines en poésie," special issue, *Palabres: Revue d'études africaines* (2001): 87–106.

4. *Dictionnaire de l'Ancienne Langue Française et de tous les dialectes du IX au XV siècle; Grand Larousse de la langue française; The Oxford English Dictionary,* 2nd ed.

5. Mayes, 94.

6. D'Almeida, 24.

7. *An Intermediate Greek-English Lexicon* (1889; repr., Oxford: Clarendon Press, 1961).

8. Boubacar Boris Diop, *L'Afrique au-delà du miroir* (Paris: Philippe Rey, 2007).

9. Ralph Ellison, "The Charlie Christian Story," in *Collected Essays of Ralph Ellison* (New York: Random House, 1995), 260–72.

10. I am grateful to the musicians Les Theard, a saxophone player, for this definition of reverberations, and Andy McCloud, a bass player, and T. K. Blue, a flute and saxophone player, for conversations about the tone note.

11. Doris Kadish, "Translation in Context," in *Translating Slavery: Gender and Race in French Women's Writing, 1783–1823* (Kent, Ohio: The Kent State University Press, 1994). Also, for a translation of a poem in English by Wheatley into Wolof, see Daouda Ndiaye, "Sang," in *Meissa and the Words Masters: Back to Africa* (Paris: Africart/Planet Woo-Comet Music, 2007). Wheatley's poem is titled "My Lord."

12. Carole Boyce Davies, ed. *Black Women's Writing: Crossing the Boundaries* (Frankfurt: Matatu/Verlag Holger Ehling, 1989).

A RAIN OF WORDS

Mélancolie

Lorsque du fond de mon abîme
J'aspire au grand jour,
Il est comme un poids énorme
Qui me rejette dans mon abîme.

Lorsque au plus profond de moi
S'allume le désir d'enfanter,
Il est comme une désillusion
Qui balaie toutes mes espérances.

Lorsque du fond de mon cœur
Renaît le Bonheur d'aimer
Il est comme un obstacle implacable
Qui m'interdit ce nouveau bonheur.

Lorsque du fond de la nuit
Mes rêves réalisent mes espoirs
Il est comme un matin insouciant
Qui me révèle la triste réalité.

Ma poupée

Mon cœur chavire de joie,
Tant il fond
A la vue
De ton minois adorable.

BERTHE-EVELYNE AGBO (BENIN)

Agbo was born in 1949 in Benin. She attended primary and secondary schools in France, at Touraine. She went to Senegal for university studies, receiving a degree in modern foreign languages from the University of Dakar. She currently lives in France.

Melancholy

When from the depth of my abyss
I reach for the broad day
It is as if a huge weight
Drags me back into my abyss.

When from the deepest part of me
The desire to bear a child burns
It is as if a disillusion
Sweeps my hope away.

When from the bottom of my heart
The Bliss of love is renewed
It is as if an immovable obstacle
Forbids new joy.

When from the bottom of night
My dreams turn to hope
It is as if a morning, indifferent,
Reveals the sad reality.

My Baby Doll

My heart so flooded with joy
Dissolves
At the sight
Of your adorable little face.

Tu dors, petite merveille,
Dans tes draps brodés au fil vert,
Tes cils délicatement ourlés,
Posés sur tes joues rondelettes.

Du fond de ton sommeil,
Tu as senti ma présence;
Tu t'es éveillée, petite chatte,
Et au jeu aussitôt tu t'es mise.

Et je te regarde te trémousser
Dans ton berceau, ignorant mon regard,
Tu fais le dos rond
Et tu bâilles à grand bruit.

Tu parles, tu lèves les bras
Tu t'étires dans ton lit.
Ça y est: ta tête s'est dressée
Et tu me regardes, étonnée.

Vas-tu me prendre? Me disent tes yeux bridés,
Ou vas-tu m'observer encore longtemps?
Me faut-il crier d'abord
Avant que tu ne comprennes?

Et mon cœur de mère sanglote
A la vue de tes larmes apparues,
Et je me précipite pour te prendre,
Tant tu es chaude et émouvante de candeur.

Ça y est: tu es dans me bras, blottie,
Et déjà tu babilles et me caresses la joue.
Mes bras, d'une caresse, t'entourent,
Je t'embrasse, tu me parles,

Et mon cœur chavire de joie.

You're sleeping, little marvel
In your cloth of green embroidery
Your delicately hemmed eyelashes
Resting on your little round cheeks.

From the depth of your sleep
You feel my presence;
You woke up, little kitten
And quickly started the game again.

So I watch you wiggling,
Ignoring me in your crib,
Arching your back
And yawning out loud.

You talk, you raise your arms
You stretch out in your bed.
That's it: your head lifted
You look at me astonished.

Will you pick me up? Your squinting eyes ask
Or, will you watch me a while longer?
Will I have to cry first
Before you understand?

And my mother's heart breaks
At the sight of your falling tears
And I hurry to hold you,
You, so warm and stirring with innocence.

That's it: you're in my arms, cuddled
You babble and caress my cheek.
With a tender touch I turn you in my arms
I hug you, you talk to me,

And my heart is flooded with joy.

Déception

Dès le réveil
Au lever du soleil
J'ai semé l'Amour
J'ai planté la compréhension
A la fin du jour
Au coucher du soleil
J'ai récolté le faux
J'ai récolté l'abus
Ma vie est devenue l'ombre
D'un triste souvenir
Je rêve d'amour
Je vis de chagrin
Mon cœur saigne
Mon corps se vide de sa force
Je n'ai plus d'armes
Je regorge de larmes
Et je me demande
A quand la fin du calvaire
A quand le début de la moisson

RUFINE AGBO (BENIN)

Born in 1954 in Ouidah, Benin, Agbo studied at the Collège Polytechnique Universitaire in Cotonou. Agbo has been a political activist and a member of several nongovernmental organizations and human rights groups centered in Benin. She works as a civil administrator in Cotonou.

Disillusion

From the awakening
To the rising of the sun
I sowed Love
I cultivated understanding
At the end of the day
At the setting of the sun
I gathered lies
I gathered abuse
My life turned into the shadow
Of a sad memory
I dream of love
I live on sorrow
My heart emptied
My body drained of strength
I am defenseless
Drowned by tears
And I ask myself
When does calvary end
When does the harvest begin

A toutes les femmes d'Algérie

A toutes les femmes d'Algérie
Immortelles dans nos mémoires
Tombées dans la lutte pour la liberté
A celles qui portent le hidjab
Et celles qui ne le portent pas.

Nés de la douleur, de l'espoir et de la mort
S'emballent nos sentiments
Comme les sons arrachés à la corde frénétique
Du violoniste envoûté par son instrument

Mensonges et haines font irruption
Criblent l'arrière-cour de nos illusions
Trahissent nos mythiques terreurs
Anéanties dans l'horreur

Derrière des murailles de silence
S'échafaudent d'infranchissables passerelles
Prêtant mémoire aux ruptures du temps
Tandis que font naufrage toutes les nacelles

Abreuvés de ruisseaux de larmes et de sang
Le désert hurle et la terre se fend

DOMINIQUE AGUESSY (BENIN/SENEGAL)

Born in 1937 in Cotonou, Benin, Aguessy has lived for most of her life in Senegal. She took a degree from the University of Bordeaux and advanced degrees in linguistics and sociology in Dakar. She has collected and edited books on African folklore and written on labor and industrial relations and the economic position of women in Africa. She currently lives in Belgium.

To all the women of Algeria

To all the women of Algeria
Immortal in our memories
Fallen in the struggle for freedom
For those who wear the hijab*
And for those who do not.

Born of pain, of hope and of death
Our feelings uncontrolled
Like sounds plucked from the frenetic string
Of the violinist enthralled with the instrument.

Lies and hatred erupt
Break out of the back lot of our illusions
Betray our mythic terrors
Annihilate them with dread

Behind the walls of silence
Scaffolds are built for impassable bridges
To fix memory in the ruptures of time
While all the little boats founder

Swamped in streams of tears and blood
The desert roars and the earth splits open

*Headscarf worn by some Muslim women.—EDITOR'S NOTE

Le poème poursuit son chemin

Le poème poursuit son chemin
Niché au cœur du parchemin
Elégamment buriné
D'une main ferme et décidée
Tandis que les idées
Attendent d'être délivrées
Par la vertu de l'aède
Espèrent qu'il intercède
Les amène à la vie
Sans trop de parti pris
Optera-t-il pour la simplicité,
Davantage d'exubérance, de spontanéité
Ou plus encore de retenue?
De la folie des couleurs
Au vertige des saveurs
Des combinaisons d'archipels
Ebauchent des structures sensuelles
La sève des mots ensemence les images
De multiples essais rendent témoignage
Dévoile l'essence originelle
De vagabondages sempiternels

Quand survient la passion

Quand survient la passion
Il n'est pas d'âge de raison
Ni de futur à préserver
D'inquisiteurs à déjouer

Qui s'y frotte s'y pique
Qui s'en approche s'y consume
Qui en disserte l'ignore
Qui se tait en renaît

The poem seeks its own way

The poem seeks its own way
Nestled in the parchment's heart
Elegantly inscribed
By a sure and decided hand
While ideas wait to be set free
By the force of the poet
Expecting she will intercede
Bringing them alive
Without an excess of prejudice
Will she choose simplicity,
Or more exuberance, more spontaneity
Or still more circumspection?
From the madness of colors
To the vertigo of flavors
From the combinations of archipelagos
Drafting the sensual structures
The sap of the words sows images
Multiple trials bear witness
Disclosing the singular essence
Of eternal idle wandering

When sudden passion comes

When sudden passion comes
There is no age of reason
There is no future to protect
There are no inquisitors to mislead

Who dares to touch it is stung
Who comes near it is consumed
Who speaks of it becomes ignorant
Who says nothing is reborn

Sans papiers

Tous les noyés se ressemblent
La mer mangeuse d'illusion
Engloutit le destin brisé
Des candidats à l'exil

Ombres confisquées
Au rythme des traversées
Tandis que clignotent
Les appels hantés de désespérance

Chacun décrit une ellipse
Pour faire partie du voyage
Né d'un cauchemar
Narré par un rabatteur insane

Plus rien à perdre
Quand la machine s'emballe
Broie les vies au passage
Décime des familles entières

La mort tiendra parole
Sans visage sans nom sans mémoire
Confondant le double et l'original
Pour donner du panache à la misère

L'urgence des jours d'impasse
Frappe à coups sauvages
Trahit la misère
Trop criante pour être perçue

Au plus profond
La douleur vrille
Pour réduire au silence
Ce qui subsiste
D'un semblant d'existence

La mort a fait son œuvre
Mais le deuil reste inachevé

Undocumented

All of the drowned look the same
The sea devouring illusion
Swallows the broken destiny
Of the seekers of exile

Confiscated shadows
In the rhythm of the crossings
While the haunting calls
Of desperation blink

Each one describes an ellipse
Becoming a part of the voyage
To be born of a nightmare
Told by a mad smuggler

Nothing left to lose
When the machine roars
Grinding up their lives in passing
Destroying entire families

Death keeps its word
Without face without name without memory
Confounds the duplicate with the original
To give panache to misery

The urgency of deadlocked days
Strikes with wild blows
Betraying the misery
Too glaring to be seen

At its deepest
Pain spirals down
Reducing to silence
The remains
Of a semblance of existence

Death has done its work
But the mourning continues unfinished

Je suis entrée en poésie

Je suis entrée en poésie
Comme on entre en dissidence
Contre les mouvances
L'oppression sophistiquée
Moderne et médiatisée
De la pensée unique

Je suis entrée en poésie
Comme on entre en résistance
Contre le déni de dignité
Aux plus pauvres de l'humanité
Justifiant les appareils des génocides
Pour donner au monde du spectacle

Je suis entrée en poésie
Comme on entre en rébellion
Pour dire le deuil de la mémoire
L'ignominie des exclusions
Le quotidien de la marginalité
L'épaisseur du mépris

Je suis entrée en poésie
Comme on entre en transhumance
Pour débusquer les certitudes
Les enchaînements fatidiques
Renouer les fils de l'histoire
A la vigilance de l'éveil

Ta lumière Seigneur

Ta lumière Seigneur
comme une couronne
sur ma tête
Ton souffle seigneur
au secret de l'inspiration
à l'origine de l'expression
verbale ou gestuelle

I entered poetry

I entered poetry
As you enter dissidence
Against the shifting alliances
The sophisticated oppression
Modern and media-manipulated
Of dominant thought

I entered poetry
As you enter resistance
Against the denial of dignity
To the poorest of humanity
Justifying the instruments of genocide
To stage spectacles for the world

I entered poetry
As you enter rebellion
To tell the grief of memory
The ignominy of exclusion
The commonality of the marginalized
The depth of contempt

I entered poetry
As you enter migrancy
To dislocate the certitudes
The fateful connections
To tie again the thread of history
With the vigilance of the awakening

Your Light, Lord

Your light, Lord,
like a crown
for my head
Your breath, Lord,
from the secret of inspiration
to the source of expression
word or gesture

posée telles touches de pinceau
sur le gris du quotidien
Le bris des égoïsmes
émiette en vain les réticences du mental
Ta patience retrouve
le voyageur égaré
pour le ramener à lui-même
où il se retrouve en Toi

Comme un souffle fragile

Comme un souffle fragile
comme une brise légère
emportée par son élan
l'offrande du jour
choisit le feu qui brûle
sans rien posséder
que l'attente qui le nourrit
la terre vibre sous les pas
le silence comme un manteau protecteur
distille une sorte d'absence
intervalle subtil toujours inachevé
architecture aux marges des pesanteurs
pour accueillir l'insaisissable
de la lumière

set down like the strokes of a brush
on the grayness of the everyday
The broken selfishness
in vain breaks in pieces the mind's silence
Your patience finds
the lost traveler
to bring him back to himself
where he finds himself in You

Like a Fragile Breath

Like a fragile breath
like a light breeze
carried by its own energy
the offering of the day
chooses the fire that burns
possessing nothing
but hope that nourished
the earth shakes under foot
silence like a sheltering cloak
distills a sort of absence
a subtle interval always incomplete
architecture at the edges of gravity
to welcome in the elusiveness
of the light

Si on pouvait

Si on pouvait s'en aller à la fin de son ouvrage
Comme le soleil au terme de sa course;
Si on pouvait arriver comme le jour et la nuit
A l'heure choisie par les saisons;
Si on pouvait entendre les adieux comme l'arbre
Ecoute le chant de l'oiseau qui le quitte
Qui craindrait les départs, les retours et la mort . . .

ASSAMALA AMOI (CÔTE D'IVOIRE)

Amoi was born in 1960 in Paris, France, and attended grammar school there. She moved to Abidjan, Côte d'Ivoire, and received a degree from the National University of Abidjan. She pursued graduate studies in English literature and writes poetry in English as well as French. She has published two novels, short stories and books for children as well as a book of poetry. She works as an editor for the World Health Organization in Congo-Brazzaville.

If You Could

> If you could leave when work was done
> Like the sun at the end of its day;
> If you could arrive like the day and the night
> At an hour chosen by the seasons;
> If you could hear the farewells like the tree
> Listens to the song of the migrating bird
> Who would dread departures, returns and death . . .

la lune a beau tendre l'oreille

la lune a beau tendre l'oreille
elle n'entend point
la brise dire ses secrets aux feuilles

ne te sens pas ridicule

ne te sens pas ridicule
les sages sourient aux hibiscus
les génies saluent les sauterelles

dans les yeux du hibou

dans les yeux du hibou
la lune et sa jumelle
laquelle abrite des chimères?

the moon tries hard

the moon tries hard
she cannot hear
the secrets the breeze tells the leaves

do not feel like a fool

do not feel like a fool
the wise smile at the hibiscus
the spirits greet grasshoppers

in the eyes of the owl

in the eyes of the owl
the moon and its twin
which one shelters fantasies?

NOTE: *The translations of these haiku into English are by Assamala Amoi.*

Assassins

Des lames de mots
Des mots de pierre
Des balles de mots
Tranchent dans la chair
Des sentiments nus le sang
Coule à flot
Aujourd'hui
Demain
Hier
Pour toujours ?
La porte ouverte ne se ferme plus
Les mots deviennent monstres insatiables
Ils labourent frénétiquement la chair
Saignement incontrôlable
Aujourd'hui
Demain
Hier
Pour toujours ?
Graine de mots assassins pousse
S'enracine avec férocité telle une gangrène
Et prend en otage la vie
Aujourd'hui
Demain
Hier
Pour toujours ?

KOUMÉALO ANATÉ (TOGO)

Born in 1968 in Kazaboua, Togo, Anaté was educated in Togo and Benin, earning an undergraduate degree from the University of Benin at Lomé. She did graduate work in France and received a doctorate in information sciences from the University of Bordeaux in 2004. She currently lives in Bordeaux, where she is an editor for the magazine Afiavi. Besides a book of poetry, Anaté has published a novel, a collection of short stories, and articles on subjects ranging from globalization and African women to the development of the Internet in Africa.

The Assassins

> Words like swords
> Words of stone
> Words like bullets
> Cut into the flesh
> From naked feelings blood
> Flows in a torrent
> Today
> Tomorrow
> Yesterday
> Maybe forever?
> The open door won't close
> The insatiable words become monsters
> Frantically slashing the flesh
> And bleeding uncontrollably
> Today
> Tomorrow
> Yesterday
> Maybe forever?
> From seeds, assassin words grow
> And roots spread with the ferocity of gangrene
> They hold our life hostage
> Today
> Tomorrow
> Yesterday
> Maybe forever?

Non !
Jusqu'à la nouvelle lune
De pluie et de souffle de mots
Libérant le baume de mots
Balayant les balles de mots
Pour féconder la cicatrice
D'une source d'espérance
Aujourd'hui
Demain
Et pour toujours.

L'oiseau prend son envol

L'oiseau prend son envol et part vers une destination pour l'instant inconnue / de lui / de ceux qui l'observent partir. Il reviendra peut-être un jour / peut-être jamais. Mais en aucun cas il n'oublie ceux qui restent / ceux qui ont compté pour lui. Les rencontres du chemin auront parfois l'odeur de leur présence. La beauté des contrées traversées lui rappellera l'amour des siens. Les brûlures du soleil / du vent / de la pluie / lui donneront la nostalgie du confort et de la sécurité. Mais ne lui demandez pas de revenir / de faire comme s'il n'était pas parti. Ne lui demandez pas d'expliquer ou de justifier son départ. C'est dans la logique des choses. Et c'est tout ! Qu'on le veuille ou non / dès l'instant où l'on part / on fait provisoirement ou définitivement deuil / deuil de quelqu'un / deuil de quelque chose. Qu'importe ce que veulent et disent les autres / qu'importe le temps que dure l'envol ! Il ne se fixera que lorsqu'il aura trouvée l'arbre / son arbre lui permettant de vivre et de s'accomplir. Malgré les apparences on sait rarement pourquoi on part. Pourtant on trouve des raisons pour le nouveau choix qui permet d'avancer / d'aller au bout de soi / au bout du monde en se laissant guider par la Source.

No!
Only until
The new moon
Of the rain and breath of words
Will free the words that soothe
Words as bullets will be swept away
The scar fertilized
A source of hope
Today
Tomorrow
Yesterday
And forever.

The bird takes flight

The bird takes flight to a destination still unknown / to him /
to those who watch him leave. He will return one day perhaps /
perhaps never. But under no circumstance will he forget those left
behind / those who have mattered to him. The meetings along the
way sometimes will have the scent of their presence. The beauty
of the countries he crosses will remind him of the love of his own
people. The burning of sun / of wind / of rain / will give him a
nostalgia for comfort and safety. But don't ask him to return / to
pretend he has never left. Don't ask him to explain or to justify his
leaving. It is in the logic of things. And that is all! Whether you
want it or not / the moment that you leave / you are in mourning
provisionally or finally / mourning for someone / mourning
for something. It doesn't matter what the others want and say /
it doesn't matter how long the flight will last! He will not alight
until he has found the tree / his tree allowing him to live and be
fulfilled. Despite appearances rarely do you know why you leave.
Yet you find reasons for the new choice that allow you to move
ahead / to go to the end of yourself / to the end of the world while
letting yourself be guided by the Source.

Les amants

Se taire et dans l'élan
Serrer l'autre contre son cœur
Donner ce qu'on n'a pu recevoir
Et dans la communion
Recevoir ce qu'on a pu demander
L'heure n'est plus à la parole
malade de dire
Le corps vibre et se rebiffe
Dans l'attente des gestes du souvenir

Se couler et se fondre pour un instant
Dans la chanson de deux êtres qui se rassurent
Oubliant ceux qui jugent et se déjugent
Et retrouver la tiédeur d'une brise aux narines

S'émouvoir d'un chant d'oiseau
des ciels d'automne dans les banlieues crasses,
dans les aéroports des grandes villes
Où Brel chante les amants
Ceux qui s'aiment et qui se quittent
jusqu'à la limite du rêve

Egréner la chanson du levant, silence du moment

EDWIGE ARABA APLOGAN (BENIN)

Born in 1955 in Porto-Novo, the political capital of Benin, Aplogan studied law in France and worked as a lawyer in Paris from 1981 to 1994. She returned to Cotonou to continue practicing law, but within in a few years resigned her position to concentrate on writing and painting. Her painting has been widely exhibited in Africa, Europe, and Latin America. She lives in Benin.

The Lovers

To remain silent and just run
To hold the other against your heart
To give what you could not receive
And in the communion
Receive what you could not ask for
The time for words is past
Sick of words
The body shivers and rebels
Anticipating the remembered gestures

To flow and melt together for a moment
In the song of two beings who reassure each other
Forgetting who judges and who does not
And recover the warmth of a breeze in the nostrils

Moved by a bird's song
in autumn skies in squalid suburbs,
in airports in big cities
Where Brel sings of lovers
Those who love and leave each other
at the end of the dream

Play the song of sunrise, the silent moment

Demain l'Afrique, L'Afrique demain

J'erre déjà
j'erre encore
j'erre cent ans
Je me réveille les yeux fermés
les yeux encore dedans
dedans-dehors.

Hordes d'affamés
sans quartiers,
sans papiers,
sans encore
sans dehors.
Les normes,
L'ascenseur.

La tête dans les cheveux,
les cheveux dans les yeux,
les yeux au creux de ma main,
je dors.
Je dors tout yeux dehors
je dors encore.

L'autre monde pleure,
se dissout, se désintègre,
demain l'Afrique

Le monde d'en dessous
le monde d'en haut
le monde d'en bas
le monde des va-t-en-guerre qui ne partent pas

Des va-t-en-guerre d'une paix octroyée
(d'une paix silence)
paix d'une enfance spoliée

Quelle fureur me guide?
quelle éternité me guette?
quelle transe me galvanise?

Regarde,
regarde le miroir pleurer.

Tomorrow Africa, Africa Tomorrow

I wander now
I wander still
I wander for one hundred years
I wake up with eyes closed
Eyes still inside
Inside-outside

Famished hordes
without home,
without papers,
still without
still outside.
Norms,
The elevator.

Head in the hair,
hair in the eyes,
eyes in the palm of my hand,
I sleep.
I sleep eyes outside in
I sleep again.

The other world cries,
dissolves, disintegrates,
tomorrow Africa

The world underneath
the world above
the world below
the world of the chosen-for-war who will not go.

Of the chosen-for-war from a given peace
(of a silent peace)
peace of a plundered childhood

What fury guides me?
what eternity waits for me?
what trance electrifies me?

Look,
look at the crying mirror.

L'enfant

L'enfant d'en haut
L'enfant d'en bas
L'enfant du désir oublié
L'enfant d'amour et de mystère
L'enfant boule, l'enfant fou
L'enfant loup
L'enfant torture
L'enfant d'un rêve retrouvé

D'un demain qui s'annonce
pour vous
pour nous
pour eux

Une étreinte
Flamme
Désir

Nous chevaucherons les déserts
d'aventures en aventures
des terres rouges aux dunes bleues
des forteresses arrachées au silence

Nous prendrons la rive d'eau claire
de pas de guerre en pas de danse
de chants d'amour et d'espérance
De vie arrachée
à la béance du présent.

The Child

Child from above
Child from below
Child of forgotten desire
Child of love and mystery
Round child, mad child
Wolf Child
Tortured Child
The child of a newfound dream

Of a tomorrow that is coming
for you
for us
for them

A tight embrace
Flame
Desire

We will ride across deserts
from one adventure to another
from red earth to blue dunes
from fortresses torn from silence

We will take over the shore of clear water
from war steps into dance steps
from songs of love and hope
Of life snatched
From the void of the present.

Marchand de femmes

Etes-vous déjà passé près de mon étal? Le marchand de femmes
est un homme qui sait vanter sa marchandise. Il faut le voir
à l'œuvre ou plutôt l'écouter : cela tient du spectacle, un peu
comme la magie, un tantinet charlatan mais terriblement
charmeur ... En effet, la réclame était si persuasive que bientôt
un tas de gens se pressaient de son côté. Il fallait voir la foule
agglutinée ... Moi-même, j'ai tenté de faire un crochet mais
comme j'étais pressée
... Et puis, cela ne devrait pas me concerner côté acheteur, il
fallait une bonne paire de moustaches. Quant à la marchandise,
je ne suis pas amatrice d'antiquité : le produit est si curieux que
je risque d'y perdre mon ... pular ! D'ailleurs, je ne sais même
plus de quel côté du marché il tient son étal. Si vous demandiez
à certains ...

Ame sœur
Oie blanche
Ma colombe
ma douce tombe

Appelez-la de tous les noms
de noms doux, de noms
sucrés-miel, beurre, farine

des noms de choses à manger
des noms de choses à caresser
des noms de choses à fouler aux pieds
Appelez-la de tous les noms

AMINATA ATHIÉ (MAURITANIA)

*Born in 1960 in St. Louis, Senegal, Athié is currently living in
Nouakchott, where she is a French teacher at Collège des jeunes
filles. Athié is involved in feminist organizations and works with
groups of female students to help them create their own newspapers.*

A Seller of Women

Have you passed by my stall? The seller of women is a man who
knows how to show off his merchandise. You should see him
do his thing or better still hear him: He puts on a show, almost
like magic, a little bit the con-man but terribly charming . . . In
fact, his pitch was so persuasive that a mob of people hurried to
gather around him. You would have seen the crowd packed in
there. Even I tried to stop, but I was in a hurry . . . And besides, I
could not myself be a buyer, since you had to have a good pair of
moustaches. As for the merchandise, I am not a lover of antiques:
the piece is so strange that I would risk losing my Pulaar . . .
Besides, I don't even know anymore which side of the market his
stall is on. If you were to ask certain people . . .

Sister Soul
White Goose
My dove
My Sweet Grave

Call her by every name
sweet names, names
of honey, butter, flour

names of things to eat
names of things to caress
names of things to trample
Call her by every name

La femme est bonne à posséder
La femme, un orgueil de la maison

Il faut avoir une femme
C'était un ange, la femme
Le paradis pavé de bonnes femmes

Femme-chauffage pour l'hiver
Femme-console pour ton salon
Femme-climatiseur pour nuits d'été
Femme-semence pour l'hivernage

Femme-cotonnade
Femme-limonade
Femme-pommade pour peaux malades

Appelez-la de tous les noms

La candidate-aride-impavide

Femme-statuette-têtue
Femme-à-la-langue trop pendue
Femme-sangsue-dodue
Femme-enfer-de fer

Femme-taloche
Femme-talisman
Femme-étalon

Appelez-la de tous les noms

La femme, bonne à exhiber
La femme, bijou de la maison

Il y en a de toutes les formes
Vous en avez pour tous les goûts

Femme d'or
Femme dorure
Femme-corps
Femme-cauris

The Woman is good to possess
The Woman, pride of the house

You must have a woman
She was an angel, the woman
Paradise is paved with good women

A woman-heater for winter
Woman-table for the living room
A woman-air conditioner for summer nights
Woman-seed for rainy seasons

Cotton-cloth woman
Lemonade-woman
Pomade-woman for bad skin

Call her by every name

The dry composed candidate

Stubborn-statuette woman
Chatterbox-woman
Leech-plump-woman
Hell-on-wheels-woman

Slap-woman
Talisman-woman
Stallion-woman

Call her by every name

The woman, good to display
The woman, jewel of the house

They come in all shapes
There is one for every taste

Golden woman
Gilded woman
Woman-body
Woman-cowry

Et même la femme-mauvais sort
et même la femme fossile

La femme, bonne à consoler
La femme, rebut de la maison

Je vends la femme, objet
de première nécessité

Il faut avoir une femme
C'était de la fange la femme

Elle mange
Elle boit
Elle dort
La femme a peur
Madame se pare
La femme pleure

Femme en long
Femme en large
Femme en profondeur

And even a bad-luck-woman
And even fossil-woman

The Woman, good to console
The Woman, household rubbish

I sell the woman, an object
of premium necessity

You must have a woman
She was made from the mire, woman

She eats
She drinks
She sleeps
Woman is scared
Madame adorns herself
Woman weeps

Woman of length
Woman of breadth
Woman of depth

Extraits de *Burkina Blues*

Comment convaincre avec des mots silencieux ?
Seule l'inquiétude se lit dans ce livre ouvert
Je l'enduirai d'argile blanche
Pour prendre l'apparence des fantômes
Et t'obliger à m'ensevelir
Dans les arrières boutiques de ta mémoire

Il suffit d'une croix
Pour tout effacer
Une simple croix
Et n'avoir jamais existé
Mais
La ténacité sert de barrière aux portes de ton sanctuaire
Abandonner ne fait pas partie de ton dictionnaire
Il me faut réinventer des lettres et ré-écrire cette non-histoire
A intégrer dans ta mémoire aux portes entrouvertes

J'ai dévalé des pentes abruptes
J'ai parcouru des sentiers sinueux
Pour me retrouver
Sur un chemin tortueux sans issue
A la merci des fauves

ANGÈLE BASSOLÉ-OUÉDRAOGO
(BURKINA FASO)

Bassolé-Ouédraogo was born in 1967 and raised in Abidjan. She received an MA from the University of Ouagadougou and a PhD in French from the University of Ottawa. She taught school in Burkina Faso then returned to Canada to study journalism in Montreal. She has published three books of poetry and a number of articles on francophone poetry in Africa. She now works as a journalist in Ottawa, where she is also director of Editions Malaika press.

From *Burkina Blues*

How do you convince with silent words?
Only disquietude can be read in this open book
I smear it with white clay
To take the semblance of ghosts
And I force you to bury me
In the back rooms of your memory

One cross is enough
To erase everything
One simple cross
And I never existed
But
Tenacity is a barrier to the doors of your sanctuary
Surrender is not found in your dictionary
I need to reinvent those letters and rewrite this non-history
To merge with your memory through half-opened doors

I have descended steep slopes
I have traveled on winding roads
To find myself once more
On a crooked path with no exit
At the mercy of beasts

J'ai imploré la compréhension des dieux
Pour que nos chemins se séparent
Je te retrouve assis au carrefour de ma mémoire
Avec une ténacité à désarmer
toute une armée
Les mots tarissent au fond de ma gorge
Comment te convaincre
Avec le silence de mes mots ?
Comment te dire
Que je ne puis être ?
Comment te faire admettre
Que non-lieu, je suis ?

Ce soir,
J'ai entendu sous ma fenêtre
Le chant des rafales de mitrailleuses
Mon antre s'est mis à flamber
J'ai éteint l'incendie naissant avec mes larmes

[…]

J'ai mal en ces enfants
J'ai mal en ces mères
J'ai mal en ce temps qui fuit
J'ai mal en la tombée fulgurante de la nuit
J'ai mal en ma solitude

Je veux retourner sur cette terre de liberté
Et enfouir toutes les détresses de la terre
Je veux redonner espoir et vie à ces enfants
A qui on n'a pas offert de choix
Ces enfants à qui on a imposé la vie
Leur avis n'a pas compté

Et les voilà à dormir sur des lits de fortune
Aux abords du marché de Ouagadougou
Et les voilà réduits à quémander leur quotidien
Sur les autoroutes d'Abidjan
Et on voudrait que je me contente de mon quotidien
Et on voudrait que j'écrive que tout est beau

I have implored the understanding of gods
That our paths be separate
I find you sitting once more at the crossroad of my memory
With enough tenacity to disarm an entire army
Words catch at the back of my throat
How do I convince you
With the silence of my words?
How do I tell you
That I cannot be
How do I make you admit
That I am dismissed?

This evening,
I heard below my window
The song of machine guns firing
My hiding place is engulfed in flames
I had drowned the rising fire with my tears

[...]

I ache in these children
I ache in these mothers
I ache in this passing time
I ache in the blazing fall of the night
I ache in my solitude

I want to return to that land of liberty
And bury all the distress of the earth
I want to restore hope, and life to these children
Who are offered no choice
These children on whom is imposed a life
Where their opinion does not count

And there they are asleep on makeshift beds
All around the marketplace in Ouagadougou
And there they are reduced to begging for their daily bread
On the highways of Abidjan
And someone wants me to be content with my daily bread
And wants me to write everything is beautiful

Je ne sais pas jouer
J'irai écrire
Sur la porte de leur palais
La souffrance des enfants de la rue
J'irai peindre
Sur les murs de leurs châteaux
Ma rage et ma rancœur
J'irai déverser
Dans leurs jardins luxueux
La misère des mères
J'irai troubler
Leurs doux sommeils
De mes cris
De mes révoltes
De mes colères

[...]

Nous relevons de la génération
Sacrifiée
Mais
Nous refusons de plier l'échine
Nous irons avec nos chants
Jusque dans leurs bagnes
Nous irons avec nos convictions
Jusqu'à leurs champs de morts

[...]

Il y a des mots
Dont la seule existence vous foudroie

I do not know how to play
I will write
On the door of their palaces
The suffering of street children
I will paint
On the walls of their chateaux
My rage and my bitterness
I will pour
Into their luxurious gardens
The misery of mothers
I will trouble
Their sweet sleep
With my cries
With my rebellions
With my fury

[…]

We are from
The sacrificed generation
But
We refuse to bow down
We will advance with our songs
Into their death camps
We will advance with our beliefs
Onto their killing fields.

[…]

There are words
Whose very existence strikes like lightning

Extraits de *Avec tes mots*

Ce soir
Il pleut des cordes ici
Oui des cordes avec lesquelles je m'enlace
J'ai l'âme en miettes et ta sagesse ne m'est d'aucun secours
Je voudrais écrire l'espoir avec tes mots
Mais je m'enfonce dans le marécage

[...]

Tes mots,
Je les aurai toujours tissés dans les fibres de mon corps
Pour me rappeler que quelque part,
Un jour, ailleurs, ici, peut-être

Tu m'attendras avec tes rêves d'espoir
Espoirs pour un continent sans nom
Déserté par ses enfants qui cherchent sous d'autres cieux
La terre promise par une multitude de prophètes

Ces prophètes morts
Pour avoir osé rêvé
Le rêve est un délit
Puni par les lois de la jungle tropicale

[...]

Tes mots ciselés de fine pointe
Qui écorchent mon âme en furie
Ma douleur silencieuse
Douleur vive face à un continent de silence

Silence au cœur de tes mots rebelles
Qui interpellent nos consciences endormies
Ebranlées par la peur
Peur d'affronter ces cannibales déguisés en démocrates

[...]

From *With Your Words*

This evening
It's pouring ropes of rain here
Yes, ropes in which I am entangled
My soul in tatters and your wisdom does not help
I want to write hope with your words
But I am slowly sinking into the swamp.

[...]

Your words,
I will have woven always into the fibers of my body
To remind me that somewhere,
Someday, elsewhere, here, maybe

You will wait for me with your dreams of hope
Hope for a continent without a name
Deserted by her children who seek under other skies
The land promised by a multitude of prophets

These prophets died
For having dared dreamed
Dreaming is an offense
Punished by laws of the tropical jungle

[...]

Your finely chiseled words
That skin my furious soul
My silent pain
Sharp pain before a silent continent

Silence at the heart of your rebellious words
That call out to our sleeping conscience
Shaken by fear
Fear to confront these cannibals disguised in democrats

[...]

Angèle Bassolé-Ouédraogo

Un continent tue
Et enterre ses enfants
Sous le regard médusé du monde

Héros d'un jour
Martyrs d'une vie
Vie gâchée à vouloir faire le bien
Faire le bien sur une terre où le mal est roi
Triste et incroyable histoire

Lumumba !
Sankara !
Ces noms résonnent
Comme autant de tambours

Tambours parlants dans nos consciences endormies
Consciences endormies de peur
De honte
De lâcheté

Sankara
Etre intègre dans un monde de dupes
Lumumba
Liberté pour un peuple enchaîné

Un peuple enchaîné
Enchaîné
Et sourd
Sourd
A l'écho des mots

A continent kills
And buries its children
Beneath the stony gaze of the world

Heroes for a day
Martyrs for a life
Life ruined striving for the good
For the good in a land where evil is king
Sad and incredible story

Lumumba!
Sankara!
These names resound
like many, many drums

Drums that talk to our sleeping conscience
Conscience lulled by fear
by shame
by cowardice

Sankara
A person of integrity in a world of dupes
Lumumba
Freedom for a people in chains

A people in chains
In chains
And deaf
Deaf
To the resonance of words

Ile mère

La cascade chante
La mélodie des vagues
Qui enlacent les basaltes
Noir argent de mon île
Silencieuse
Qui au large de Dakar
Garde son mystère
Gorée ma belle
Ton image ancrée en moi
Fredonne la mélodie du
Souvenir et des larmes
Gorée ma stoïque
Ton souvenir
Me rappelle le calvaire
De tant de générations perdues
Dans la braise du sang et de la haine
Gorée île-mère
Qui demeure le flambeau de ma propre destinée.

—*Le 18 mai 2002*

SOKHNA BENGA (SENEGAL)

Benga was born in 1967 in Dakar, where she attended local schools and matriculated at the University Cheikh Anta Diop. She went to France and attended the University of Bretagne in Brest, specializing in maritime law. She has published a book of poetry, five novels, a novella, coauthored a script for a children's film, and written various technical papers on maritime regulation. She currently works as an administrator of maritime affairs in Dakar.

Mother Island

The falling water sings
The melody of waves
Embracing the dark silver
Basalt of my island of
Silence
That, off the coast of Dakar,
keeps its mystery
Gorée my beautiful
Your image anchored in me
Hums the melody of
Memory and of tears
Gorée my stoic
Your memory
Calls me back to the Calvary
Of many many generations lost
In the embers of blood and of hatred
Gorée mother-island
You remain the flame of my own fate.

Palestine

Palestine
Tu pleures tes morts de l'Intifada
Martyrs au regard sans lumière
Dont le sang tapissé
D'un drap vermeil
La terre qui a vu naître
tant de porteurs d'espoirs

Palestine
De tes entrailles
Surgissent
Les hurlements des suppliciés
Sur l'autel de l'injustice
Les cris des kamikazes
Aux yeux vitreux

Palestine
Nous pleurons avec toi

—*Le 18 mai*

Palestine

Palestine
You lament your dead of the Intifada
Martyrs with a lightless gaze
Whose blood has covered
With a red cloth
The land that saw the birth
Of so many bearers of hope

Palestine
From your bowels
Rise
The howls of the tortured
Upon the altar of injustice
The cries of the kamikazes
With their glazed eyes

Palestine
We cry with you.

Voyage

(Pour cors et balafon)

J'ai pourtant voyagé
Dans d'autres galaxies
Mais l'on viendra ici
Refaire l'ordalie
Qu'importe . . .

J'ai beaucoup voyagé
Dans d'autres galaxies
A des années-lumière
Depuis des millénaires
J'ai traversé les espaces déserts
Et les gouffres amers
J'ai parcouru les ciels
Et l'enfer

Dans des grottes marines
Je me suis arrêtée
Sur des tours infernales
J'ai longtemps séjourné
J'ai franchi des torrents
Qui charriaient le sang
Tumulte prodigieux
Au milieu des rochers

Je me riais du vent
Qui s'engouffrait hurlant
Dans des abîmes géants

THÉCLA G. BÉNISSAN (BENIN)

Bénissan was born in 1947. She received her initial education in Togo's capital, Lomé. Her university education was continued in France, where she received a doctorate in general and comparative literature. She is currently a professor at the Université d'Abomey-Calavi, Benin. Bénissan has a number of scholarly publications but is best known for her writing for children.

Voyage

(With horns and balafon*)

And yet I have traveled
Into other galaxies
But we will come here
To face again the ordeal
Whatever it might be . . .

I have traveled a great deal
In other galaxies
Light-years away
Since time immemorial
I have crossed deserted landscapes
and the bitter abyss
I have traversed all over heaven
and hell

Into deep-sea grottoes
I have stopped
On infernal towers
I have stayed
I have crossed rushing waters
That carried along the blood
Enormous turbulence
Between two cliffs

I mocked the wind
That rushed howling
Into gigantic abysses

Creusés par les volcans
J'ai descendu le fleuve
Qui conduit au séjour des Morts
Et sur ses rives lointaines
Des fantômes grimaçants
M'appelaient de la main

J'ai traversé l'éther
J'ai vu d'autres planètes
Et tel le météore
J'ai croisé
De phosphorescentes comètes

Roc Arbre Vent
Je me suis fondue dans l'atmosphère
Eclair Foudre Tonnerre
J'ai précédé la tempête
Et me suis apaisée aux Séjours Divins

Sonnez Clairons et Olifants
Que votre souffle me porte
Et m'emporte plus loin
Toujours plus loin
Sumériens Ethiopiens Nubiens
Sauriens Hippocampes Astres
Me reconnaissez-vous
Je suis devenue FEMME

J'ai beaucoup voyagé
Dans d'autres galaxies
A des années-lumière
Depuis des millénaires
Mais l'on viendra ici
Refaire l'ordalie
Qui me condamnera
Pour toujours
A cette éternité !

Gouged by volcanoes
I have descended the river
That led to the home of the Dead
And on these distant shores
Grimacing phantoms
Beckoned to me

I have passed through ether
I have seen other planets
And like the meteor
I have passed by
Phosphorous comets

Rock Tree Wind
I have melted into the atmosphere
Lightning-bolts Lightning Thunder
I preceded the storm
And calmed myself in Divine Dwellings

Blow the Trumpets and Ivory horns
So that your breath carries
And bears me farther
Ever farther
Sumerians Ethiopians Nubians
Saurian Hippocampus Stars
Do you recognize me
I have become WOMAN

I have traveled often
To other galaxies
Light-years away
Since time immemorial
But we come here
To face again the ordeal
That will condemn me
Forever
To this eternity!

Percussive musical instrument (also spelled balaphon*) found in West Africa, resembling a xylophone.*—EDITOR'S NOTE

Gorée, mon île

(Pour koras)

Ile lointaine perdue dans la brume
Plages de sable fin et collines de granit
Gorée mon île perdue au fond de l'Océan
Tu fus choisie parmi les îles

Plages de sable fin et collines de granit
Combien de fils d'Afrique avez-vous vu partir
Pour ne jamais revenir
Gorée mon île choisie parmi les îles

Enchaînés au fond des caves
Enchaînés au fond des cales
Combien furent-ils jetés à l'eau à fond de cales
Gorée mon île perdue parmi les îles

Voici la Maison des Esclaves
Et là-bas la mer étale
Voici l'Ecole Normale et les Canons de Navaronne
L'horrible commerce de l'Auberge du Chevalier

Gorée mon île voici aussi le Chant du Souvenir
Pour calmer tes blessures oublier les injures
Ecoute le Chant du Souvenir
Gorée mon île choisie parmi les îles

Gorée, My Island

(For kora*)

Distant island lost in the mist
Beaches of fine sand and granite hills
Gorée, my island lost at the end of the Ocean
You were chosen among islands.

Beaches of fine sand and granite hills
How many children of Africa have you seen depart
Never to return
Gorée, my chosen island among islands

Chained at the bottom of cellars
Chained at the bottom of holds
How many were thrown from the holds into the water
Gorée, my island lost among islands

Here is La Maison des Esclaves
And there the resting sea
Here is the Teachers' College and the Canons of Navaronne
The hideous commerce of the Auberge du Chevalier.

Gorée, my island here also is the Song of Memory
To ease your wounds forget the abuses
Listen to the Song of Memory
Gorée, my chosen island among islands.

*West African musical instrument with twenty-one to twenty-six strings.
—EDITOR'S NOTE

Bidonvilles

Voici la Liberté enchaînée
Jusqu'à la moelle !
Dans les marais puants
Dans les poubelles de la ville
Dans les crottes de porc
Qui engraissent les plantes-et-les-fleurs-à-papa !
La liberté est là
Noyée étouffée jusqu'aux os
Tremblante de froid de peur
De chaleur humaine
Comprimée
Compressée
Balancée dans la marge
Sous un bananier rêveur
Qui écrit en grosses lettres vertes
L'histoire des sous-hommes et demi
Virus indésirables
Qui grouillent vers la vie
Dans la plaie de la ville
Ils ne désirent qu'un peu de soleil !

TANELLA BONI (CÔTE D'IVOIRE)

One of the most prominent poets and writers of francophone
Africa, Boni was born in 1954 in Abidjan and completed her early
education there. She went to France for university studies, beginning
at Toulouse and then completing a doctorate of philosophy at the
Sorbonne. She taught philosophy at the University of Abidjan,
where she also organized the Abidjan International Poetry Festival.
The first of her five books of poetry was published in 1984, and she
has also published short stories, books for children, four novels, and
numerous essays and critical works. She is now living in France.

Shantytowns

Here is Liberty squeezed
To the very marrow!
In the stinking swamps
In the trash piles of the city
In the pig dung
Fattening the bourgeois gardens
Liberty is there
Drowned stifled to the bone
Shivering from cold from fear
With human heat
Repressed
Crushed
Pushed to the margins
Beneath a dreaming banana tree
That writes in huge green letters
The tale of the sub- and the half-human
Undesirable viruses
That swarm toward life
Inside the city's open sore
Wanting only a little sun!

Extraits de *Grains de sable*

Tous les jours qui passent elles empruntaient
par voie de rupture en diagonale les chemins
de fracture comme des mains magnifiques
ressemblant étrangement à celles du voyageur
elles faisaient irruption dans l'atmosphère
assassinée à coup de bombes aérosols alors
la couche d'ozone pour une seconde vivait à
pleins poumons après les terribles décharges
électriques infligées çà et là par les soins
d'électrodes-cerveaux pour une seconde elles
voilaient l'immondice des déchets toxiques
pour une seconde elles tamisaient en gerbes
liées les grains de sable du désert alors ils
comprirent que la Femme c'est comme la
pluie elle fabrique l'oxygène du Temps

[…]

Si tu n'étais pas n'étais point l'homme
t'aurait fabriquée comme une poupée comme
un jouet et tu es et tu es et tu es pour
le bonheur la surnature de l'homme de
l'homme de l'homme et tu es et tu dors
et tu meurs dans les bras de feu de mots
de l'homme il court il court avec toi il
court sans toi et tu es et tu es née et tu
meurs sur l'estomac d'un nom d'homme
nom de père nom d'époux et tu nais nom
de puce pucelle et tu meurs épouse
mortelle et tu brûles de feu de mots de
jeu de vie de vie de dé à gagner à hériter
à partager à renflouer et tu es l'or perdu
l'or retrouvé de tous les fleuves du monde

From *Grains of Sand*

All the days that pass   they walked
to see the diagonal rupture   the ways
of breaking   like the magnificent hands
strangely similar to those   of the traveler
they irrupted into   the atmosphere
murdered by a blast of aerosol sprays   then
the ozone layer   lived for a second with
full lungs   after the terrible discharges of
electricity   inflicted here and there   thanks to
the electrode-brains   for a second they
hid   the filth of toxic wastes
for a second they sifted   in sheafs
tied the grains of desert sand   then they
understood that Woman   is like
rain   she creates the oxygen of Time

[...]

If you were not   were not   man
would have made you   like a doll like
a toy   and you are and you are and you are   for
the happiness   the super-nature of man   of
man   of man   and you are and you sleep
and you die   in the arms of word fire
of man   he runs he runs with you   he
runs without you   and you are and you are born and you
die   on the stomach of a man's name
name of a father name of a husband and you are born name
of a flea   a virgin flea   and you die married
mortal   and you burn from a fire of words   from
a game of life of life of chance   to win to inherit
to share to salvage   and you are lost gold
gold retrieved   from all the rivers of the world

Extraits de *Il n'y a pas de parole heureuse*

Où trouver le mot juste
De la porte du silence
Pour ouvrir la danse du conte
Près de ma peau de femme
Que le bon Dieu a inventée
Comme un instrument de musique inédite

[...]

Tu vois
Je ne sais pas chiffrer les odeurs
Je ne sais pas trier les couleurs
Ma mémoire mélange la matière
Avec laquelle je vais créer
L'homme et la femme rêvés

            Car
                                le
                Pays
    réel
                                                explose
            en
                mille
                morceaux

Le pays réel retombe
A l'Etat de magma merdique
Ce double M au carré

From *There Are No Happy Words*

Where to find the perfect word
For the door of silence
To open the dance of the story
Next to my woman's skin
That God created
As an instrument of unpublished music.

[...]

You see
I don't know how to count odors
I don't know how to sort colors
My memory mixes the matter
With which I will create
the man and the woman of dreams

       Because

                           the

            real

  Country

                                      explodes

    into

         a thousand
         pieces

The real country returns to
The state of magma and *merde*
This double M squared.

Extraits de *Chaque jour l'espérance*

signer la lettre à la mer
royaume des misères
et parvis des bonheurs
sur le pas étale du sable
car la lettre à la mer
a ouvert la porte du silence
là où je partage
les étoiles de ma peau
avec l'auréole de ton corps

[...]

seuls les mots racontent
des poussières de joie
les mots tissent
passerelle et vie commune
en milliers d'étoiles
sur les rives étales
de ma peau plurielle
des milliers de mots
forment l'écume du silence
qui balaie au lever du jour
nos îles mutines
étrangères l'une à l'autre
comme deux parallèles
qui n'ont jamais rien à se dire
le silence des mots conte
le souffle de l'aurore
qui précède nos pas
là où la parole d'hier n'a rien à dire

car il faut emprunter les ruelles du silence
pour habiter la liberté du jour à venir

[...]

From *The Hope of Every Day*

signing the letter to the sea
kingdom of misery
and sacred space of happiness
upon the smooth step of sand
for the letter to the sea
has opened the door of silence
there where I share
stars of my skin
with the glow of your body

[...]

only words tell stories
of grains of joy
words weave
bridge and communal life
into thousands of stars
across the still shore
of my multiple skin
of the thousands of words
forming the foam of silence
that at daybreak sweeps
over our mutinous islands
strangers to each other
like two parallel lines
with nothing to say between them
the silence of words narrates
the breath of dawn
preceding our footsteps
to where words spoken yesterday have nothing to say

for we need to travel the backways of silence
to dwell in the freedom of the coming day

[...]

la vie d'ouvrier est un chapeau
perméable à la pluie
et ces bras porteurs d'espoir
et ce visage tendu vers le vert
infiniment vert de la feuille miracle
l'ouvrier conte sa vie de labeur
de souffrance
sa vie patience
sa vie soleil et pluie
l'ouvrier cache la parole en pointillé
entre les nervures de la feuille miracle
l'ouvrier conte l'humeur de la Terre
et les vents du cyclone
l'ouvrier ne gagne pas sa vie
il la tisse en paroles
de la Terre et du ciel
il travaille aux fenêtres du Temps
afin que le Bon Dieu
admire sa silhouette de misère

[...]

à la mémoire des enfants d'Icare
disparus en plein vol
les nouveaux adultes
métamorphosés en papillons
inventent des jeux d'enfants inattendus
afin que la Terre d'Afrique
rassemble les chemins de traverse
qui nous habitent
car il suffit d'un coup d'aile de papillon
pour déclarer la guerre au chaos

the life of the worker is a hat
the rain soaks through
and these arms carrying hope
and this taut face lifting up towards the green
infinitely the green of the miracle leaf
the worker tells his life of labor
of suffering
his patient life
his sun and rain life
the worker hides words in engravings
among the nerves of the miracle leaf
the worker tells the disposition of the Earth
and the cyclonic winds
the worker does not earn his living
he weaves it into words
of Earth and sky
he works at the windows of Time
so that the Good Lord
can admire his silhouette of Misery

[…]

in memory of the children of Icarus
vanished in midflight
new adults
metamorphosed into butterflies
inventing unheard of children's games
so that the Earth of Africa
gathers the crossroads
that live within us
because the flutter of a butterfly wing is enough
to declare war on chaos

Extraits de *Gorée, île baobab*

je pose le pas pour la millième fois
sur les marches de l'escalier croissant de lune
je vais honorer les dieux qui veillent encore
la porte du non-retour

           combien étaient-elles
           fenêtres du silence
           enchaînées par la force des bras
           et la couleur de la peau

[…]

ici Jo Ndiaye a donné la parole
aux murs du silence qui disent le temps
des horreurs oubliées

           et les murs lavés à l'eau de mer
           immense et noire
           égrènent à l'infini les mots passage et traversée
           de l'homme à la bête de somme

et les murs incrustés de pierres
content encore les cris et les prières
du sel porteur d'espérance

[…]

Gorée baobab porte du continent
jeté dans la marge sans fin
par la faute de nos mains
oublieuses de la ficelle et du lien

Gorée carrefour baobab aux racines étales
et pourtant mémoire indivisible de traces et barbarie
soumises à la rondeur des siècles sur peau de mer
chaque jour renouvelée

           comme l'amour de toi m'habite
           immense inconsolable

           toi l'inséparable séparé

From *Gorée, Baobab Island*

I put my foot for the thousandth time
on the steps of the crescent moon staircase
I will honor the gods who still watch over
the door of no return.

> How many were there
> windows of silence
> Bound in chains by brute force
> and the color of the skin

[...]

here Jo Ndiaye* has given a voice
to the walls of silence that tell of the times
of forgotten horrors

> and the walls washed by the waters of the sea
> immense and black
> tell, until infinity, the words of passage and of crossing over
> from man to beast of burden

and the walls encrusted with stones
still recount the cries and the prayers
of the salt that carries hope

[...]

Gorée baobab gate of the continent
thrown into the endless margins
by the failure of our hands
forgetful of the thread and the tie

Gorée baobab crossroad with spreading roots
yet, with an indivisible memory of traces and barbarity
subjected to the cycle of centuries across the skin of the sea
every day renewed

> like your love that fills me
> immense and inconsolable

> you the separated inseparable

69   Tanella Boni

[…]

c'est ici que j'ouvre la boîte sans fond
de nos maux séculaires
je ne sais plus si tu es là toi abysse et volcan
par-delà toutes les éclipses qui pèlent ma peau

viens île baobab aux bras nus
comme Gorée mémoire de toute traversée
viens voir le point de jonction entre la terre et le ciel

ici se tisse sous nos pas
sous nos yeux la première marche
le premier mot qu'accompagnent
la souffrance et l'espérance

Extraits de *Ma peau est fenêtre d'avenir*

car tes mains saignent encore de devoir
serrer d'autres mains tissées de ruse
rivées aux sources de la déchirure des voix
seul lieu qui panse en gerbe nos plaies
où suppure la haine de l'autre

mais ta peau ne dort pas
à l'ombre des maux du monde

ta peau est fenêtre d'avenir
vers un lointain futur
dont tu traces les lignes
avec la fine pointe de tes yeux

[...]

here I open the bottomless void
of our secular evils
I no longer know if you are there you abyss and volcano
beyond the eclipses that flay my skin

come baobab island with naked arms
like Gorée memory of every passage
come see the meeting point of earth and sky

        here woven under footsteps
        under our eyes the first step
        the first word accompanied by
        suffering and hope

Boubacar Joseph Ndiaye is the well-known Senegalese oral historian and curator at La Maison des Esclaves on Gorée Island. Since the time of independence in Senegal, Jo Ndiaye has guided throngs of visitors to this historical site of horror, terror, and brutality, from which African men, women, and children were dispersed through "The Door of No Return," a loaded symbol of departure into slavery.

From *My Skin Is Window to the Future*

because your bleeding hands must still
grip other hands woven of deception
riveted to the sources of torn voices
the only place that dresses our wounds in bouquets
where the hatred of the other festers

but your skin does not sleep
in the shadow of the world's evils

your skin is a window to the future
to a distant future
whose lines you trace
with the sharp point of your eyes.

et tu parles encore du monde
et tu dis Terre ô Terre habitable
sans frontière à fleur de peau humaine

aujourd'hui ton pays
le plus beau de la carte du cœur

ton pays
se fracture se disloque
ton pays se volatilise

et tu poursuis lueurs et ruelles
étincelles qui n'ont pas cours ici-bas
et tu marches sans relâche à hauteur de femme
parmi les décombres des cœurs en miettes

[…]

je continue d'offrir ma peau en partage
au soleil à la mer au vent qui vient
à la pluie inattendue
ma peau sans couleur parce qu'elle est couleur
sans qualité couleur tout court

ma peau qui va si bien à toute toile
à tout poème à toute parole

comme étincelles d'espoir
dans la nuit de vos mots assassins

[…]

car je serai la dernière femme
dessinée à fleur de peau la dernière femme
espoir sans café sans cacao
trésors de guerre depuis des siècles

je serai la dernière femme
née du rêve de l'ombre
libérant l'étincelle
dans l'attente de demain

and still you speak of the world
and you say Earth o inhabitable Earth
without superficial human borders

today, your country
the most beautiful on the map of the heart

your country
is broken is dismembered
your country dissolves

and you pursue glimmers and pathways
sparks that have no relevance on this earth
and you march steadily towards the heights of women
amid the debris of broken hearts

[…]

I continue to offer my skin in a sharing
to the sun to the sea to the wind that comes
to the unexpected rain
my skin without color is color
color simply without quality

my skin that goes so well with every cloth
with every poem with every speech

like sparks of hope
in the night of your assassin words

[…]

because I will be the last woman
barely sketched, the last woman
hope without coffee without cocoa
treasures of war for centuries

I will be the last woman
born of the shadow's dream
freeing fires
Waiting for tomorrow

L'enfant près du rivage

Aboliga the Frog one day brought us a book of freaks and oddities, and showed us his favorite among the weird lot. It was a picture of something the caption called an old manchild.—Ayi Kwei Armah

Sur la rive
Un enfant regardait l'immensité
Les vagues sans cesse renouvelées
Semblaient le fasciner
Il était seul
L'enfant près du rivage
Je l'appelai
Il demeura immobile
Ma voix doucement se fit plus forte
Il se retourna sombre grave
Visage de parchemin
Terni par de grands yeux
Où
Jamais
Le soleil n'avait brillé
J'y décelai une ombre
De profonde souffrance
Famine fatigue peines chaînes
Avaient fait de lui
Un enfant de quatre-vingts ans
Vers lui j'ai tendu la main
Il n'a pas voulu la prendre
Je lui ai parlé
Il n'a pas voulu répondre

IRÈNE ASSIBA D'ALMEIDA (BENIN/USA)

*Born in 1945 in Dakar, Senegal, d'Almeida was educated in
Benin, Senegal, Nigeria, France, and the United States, where
she earned a doctorate in comparative literature from Emory
University in Atlanta. Besides publishing poetry in French and
English, d'Almeida has written extensively on francophone women's
literature in Africa. Since 1989 she has lived in Tucson, where she is
Professor of French at the University of Arizona.*

The Child on the Shore

*Aboliga the Frog one day brought us a book of freaks and oddities, and
showed us his favorite among the weird lot. It was a picture of something
the caption called an old manchild.*—Ayi Kwei Armah

> On the shore
> A child stared into immensity
> The waves repeating without end
> Seemed to absorb him
> He was alone
> The child on the shore
> I called to him
> He did not move
> Gently I raised my voice
> He turned to me a somber grave
> Face of parchment
> With large dull eyes
> Where
> Never
> The sun had shone
> I discovered a shadow
> Of profound suffering
> Hunger exhaustion chains pain
> Made him
> An eighty-year-old child
> I held out my hand
> He would not take it
> I spoke to him
> He would not answer

J'ai souri puis j'ai ri
Son vieux visage d'enfant
Comme le poing du nouveau-né
Est resté fermé
J'étais venue trop tard

Vagues de plaisir

Tu ne sauras jamais
La joie profonde
De la femme
Satisfaite
Au tréfonds de son corps
Après la tendre caresse
De l'amant

Dans le vertige de l'extase
Ses perles aux reins
Deviennent chanson
Ondoyante de désir
Tout son corps
Devient frisson
Hissée sur des sommets insoupçonnés
Arc-boutée de plaisir
Elle est bientôt
Mer étale
Et même dans l'abandon
Sa petite mort reste somptueusement vivante
Après, bien après le sommeil
Après, bien après le réveil

Tu ne sauras jamais
La joie profonde
De la femme
Satisfaite
Au tréfonds de son corps
Après la tendre caresse
De l'amant

I smiled then I laughed
His old-man child's face
Like a newborn's fist
Remained closed
I was too late

Waves of Pleasure

You will never know
The profound joy
Of a woman
Satisfied
In the innermost depth of her body
After the tender touch
Of her lover

Dizzy in ecstasy
Her waist beads
Become song
Swaying with desire
Her whole body
Shivering
Rising over undreamed mountains
Arched with pleasure
She is soon
A sea becalmed
Still drifting
Her little death still sumptuously alive
After, long after sleep
After, long after awakening

You will never know
The profound joy
Of a woman
Satisfied
In the innermost depth of her body
After the tender touch
Of her lover

Afrique

Je me suis laissé dire
Que l'Afrique était belle
Comme les grandes femmes du Sahel
A la peau de bronze
Et aux cheveux de jais

Je me suis laissé dire
Que l'Afrique était forte
De ses hommes d'antan
Fiers et valeureux guerriers
De ses amazones belliqueuses
De ses charmes et de ses talismans

Je me suis laissé dire
Que l'Afrique était grande
Comme le furent les Pokou Amina Nzinga Kimpa Vita
Béhanzin Samori Chaka Dan Fodio
Et tant d'autres encore

Je me suis laissé dire
Que l'Afrique était riche
Ivoire or diamants
Terres généreuses fruits en abondance

Je me suis laissé dire
Que l'Afrique était fraternelle
Que pour elle l'invité était roi
Et le seuil de l'autre sacré

Je me suis laissé dire
Que l'Afrique était sage
Qu'elle avait depuis la première lune
Accumulé la sagesse des Grands
Et qu'elle l'avait semée dans ses chants
Ses proverbes ses contes féeriques et fascinants
Et que cette sagesse avait germé
Et grandi et rejailli
Sur ses nombreux enfants

Africa

I let myself be told
That Africa was beautiful
Like tall women of the Sahel
With bronze skin
And jet black hair

I let myself be told
That Africa was strong
In men of olden times
Proud and brave warriors
In Amazon warrior women
In spells and talismans

I let myself be told
That Africa was great
As were Pokou Amina Nzinga Kimpa Vita
Béhanzin Samori Chaka Dan-Fodio
And so many more

I let myself be told
That Africa was rich
Ivory gold diamonds
Bountiful land fruits in abundance

I let myself be told
That Africa was welcoming
For her the guest was king
And all thresholds sacred

I let myself be told
That Africa was wise
That from the first moon she
Gathered the wisdom of the Ancients
And planted it in her fields of songs
Proverbs tales of magic and wonder
This germinating wisdom had
Grown and splashed
Onto her many children

Je me suis laissé dire
Que l'Afrique était droite
Que le fil des ans
Avait donné à ses Anciens
Le sens de la justice de la probité
Profond enraciné pour jamais

Je me suis laissé dire
Que l'Afrique était pure
Comme le regard limpide
De l'enfant nouveau-né

Je me suis laissé dire
Que l'Afrique était vivante
Vivante et gaie
Remplie de cris de joie
Résonnante des mains agiles qui battent avec frénésie
Des pieds souples qui martèlent la glaise
Vibrante des reins possédés par le rythme
Des dos qui ondulent
Des poitrines qui s'enflent
Des voix qui s'enflamment

Et j'ai voulu moi-même dire
Toutes ces choses de l'Afrique d'aujourd'hui
Mais je n'ai vu partout que
Faiblesse et misère
Charlatanisme et jalousie
Vol viol et vilenie
Et j'ai pleuré sur ce continent
Des larmes de douleur.

Exorcisme

Je me suis allongée
Sur le sable de perles fines
Tremblante
J'ai attendu la terrifiante mort
Elle s'est glissée en moi

I let myself be told
That Africa was honest
That the thread of years
Gave to its Elders
A sense of justice of probity
Profound rooted forever

I let myself be told
That Africa was pure
Like the clear gaze
Of a newborn child

I let myself be told
That Africa was alive
Alive and joyous
Filled with joyful cries
Resonant with agile hands drumming with frenzy
With supple feet beating the earth
Vibrant with hips possessed by rhythm
With undulating backs
With swelling chests
With voices in flames

And I myself wanted to tell
All of these things about today's Africa
But everywhere I could only see
Weakness and misery
The charlatan and the jealous
Theft rape and villainy
And over this continent I cried
Tears of pain

Exorcism

I lay down
On the fine pearly sand
Trembling
I waited for terrifying death
It slipped into me

Et nous avons fait corps
Et dans cette étreinte insolite
La Peur s'est envolée en vague nuée
Le Froid s'est transformé en pure ondée

Où est donc la légendaire frayeur?
Où est donc la légendaire froideur?

Atlantique des mille traversées

Atlantique des mille traversées
Tu as vu
des milliers de Noirs
quitter les rives de Gorée, de Ouidah, d'Elmina

Atlantique des mille traversées
Tu as vu
des milliers de Noirs
chaire à tout faire
entassée dans le ventre cupide des bateaux négriers

Atlantique des mille traversées
Tu as entendu les murmures-agonie
et les sanglots au plus profond des flots

Atlantique des mille traversées
Tu as senti
les tumultes de la mer et les tumultes de l'âme
tempêtes de terreur au fond des cœurs qui n'en savaient rien
qui n'en pouvaient mais

Et là-bas sur la Terre Autre
les affres de l'esclavage
brimades fusillades lynchages
mais aussi
RÉSISTANCE
L'être noir DEBOUT
dans toute sa splendeur
dans toute sa fierté

And we became one
In this strange embrace
Fear vanished into a vague haze
Cold evaporated into pure mist

Where now is the legendary fear?
Where now is the legendary cold?

Atlantic of a Thousand Crossings

Atlantic of a thousand crossings
You have seen
thousands of Blackpeople
leaving the shores of Gorée, of Ouidah, of Elmina

Atlantic of a thousand crossings
You have seen
Thousands of Blackpeople
their flesh for any work
packed in the greedy bowels of slaveships

Atlantic of a thousand crossings
You have heard the agonized sounds
and sobs from the profoundest deeps

Atlantic of a thousand crossings
You have felt
the tumult of the sea and the tumult of the soul
storms of terror in the depth of hearts that did not know
and could not know . . .

And there, over there in the Other World
The horrors of slavery,
persecution shooting lynching
But also
RESISTANCE
Blackness RISING
in all its splendor
in all its pride

mu par la passion du rythme
la survie-folie du chant
les negro spirituals
fendant les nuages du ciel
mu par le mythe du "Flying African"
et par la réalité du Retour

Atlantique des mille traversées
Tu as vu des milliers de Noirs
Revenir sur la Terre Ancestrale
Dubois, Wright, Baldwin,
Malcolm X, Angéla Davis,
Alex Haley, Maya Angelou . . .
Et bien d'autres encore
Aux noms ténébreux
Aux cœurs lumineux
Aux sens gourmands d'écouter de regarder
De humer de palper de goûter
L'Afrique

Atlantique des mille traversées
Tu as vu des milliers de Noirs
revenir sur la Terre Ancestrale
faisant honteusement mentir
les "Portes de non-retour" !

Atlantique-séparation
Atlantique-humiliation
Atlantique-ressentiment
Mais aussi, mais toujours
Atlantique-trait-d'union
Magnifique arc-en-mer
Jeté pour nous
entre l'Afrique et l'Amérique.

moved by the fire of rhythm
the madness of survival in song
Negro Spirituals
splitting open the cloudy skies
moved by the myth of the Flying African
and the reality of the Return

Atlantic of a thousand crossings
You have seen thousands of Blackpeople
Return to the Ancestral Land
Dubois, Wright, Baldwin,
Malcolm X, Angela Davis
Alex Haley, Maya Angelou . . .
And many more
With obscure names
With luminous hearts
With senses hungry to listen to look
to breathe to touch to taste
Africa

Atlantic of a thousand crossings
You have seen thousands of Blackpeople
return to the Ancestral Land
making shameful liars of
The "Doors of No Return"!

Atlantic-of-separation
Atlantic-of-humiliation
Atlantic-of-resentment
But also and always
Atlantic as a hyphen
Magnificent *arc-en-mer**
Cast for us
between Africa and the Americas

*The term arc-en-mer is a wordplay on arc-en-ciel, which means
a rainbow. English versions seemed inadequate, thus, the French
was retained.*

"Une femme comme il faut"

Kalifa m'a dit:
"Une femme comme il faut
Doit aimer son mari
Le trouver plus beau qu'autrui
Le bénir tous les jours
D'avoir fait d'elle une personne

Elle dit OUI, quand il tousse
BIEN, quand il rote
Et AMEN, quand il pète !

Elle accourt au moindre geste
De son doigt pointé
Et fait ceci et fait cela
Selon son vouloir bon ou mauvais !

Elle lui fait à manger
Selon son goûtt
Son goût à elle est très peu important
Elle lui sert le dessert à son goût
Son goût à elle est très peu important
Elle lui sert de dessert à treize heures
Et de souper froid à minuit
Elle flatte ainsi son palais
Son ventre et plus bas
Qu'elle le veuille ou qu'elle le veuille pas !

BERNADETTE DAO (BURKINA FASO)

Born in 1952 in Mali, Dao has spent most of her working life in Burkina Faso. She was educated at universities in Ouagadougou and Dakar, then at Ohio State and the Sorbonne. She has been a professor of French and written on the teaching of reading and literature. From the 1980s, Dao held various administrative positions in Burkina Faso, including Minister of Culture and Director of International Relations. Besides her poetry and scholarly work, Dao has published collections of short stories.

"A Proper Wife"

> Kalifa told me:
>   "A proper wife
>   Must love her husband!
>   Find him more handsome that anyone else
>   Thank him every day
>   For having made her into somebody
>
>   She says YES, when he coughs
>   GOOD, when he belches
>   And AMEN, when he farts!
>
>   She scurries at the slightest movement
>   Of his pointed finger
>   And does this and does that
>   According to his will, good or bad!
>
>   She cooks for him
>   According to his liking
>   What she likes is of very little importance
>   She serves him the dessert he likes
>   What she likes is of very little importance
>   She serves as his dessert at 1 p.m.
>   And a cold supper at midnight
>   This way she flatters his palate
>   His stomach and down below
>   Whether she wants it or not!

Une femme comme il faut
        Ecoute parler son mari
    Elle dit : OUI, à son propos douteux
            BIEN, à son rire niais
        Et AMEN, à son mot grossier!
    Elle bée d'admiration devant lui
    Et le place sur un socle d'or !

        Elle s'habille à son goût
        Son goût à elle ne compte vraiment pas
        Elle se coiffe à son goût
        Son goût à elle ne compte vraiment pas
        Elle le laisse choisir son parfum
            Et s'en réjouit très fort
            Quel qu'en soit le relent !

Une femme comme il faut
        Oublie vite "le papier"
        Et l'école qui le lui a appris
        Elle tient de son mari
Toute instruction
            Et de lui encore
                Tout jugement !
        Elle voit le monde par ses yeux
            Et par ses yeux encore
            Sa vie à elle, ses joies et ses larmes !

Une femme comme il faut
        Doit aimer son mari
            —M'a dit Kalifa mon mari—
L'aimer très fort et le bénir à toujours
    Le trouver beau et malin
            A tous propos
        S'en remettre à lui
            Et à lui seul
            Et attendre
                Béate
        Qu'Il lui porte la vie
                Et le monde !"

A proper wife
 Listens as her husband talks
 She says: YES, to his shady proposition
  GOOD, to his silly giggle
  And AMEN, to his vulgar word!
 She gapes at him with admiration
 And places him on a pedestal of gold!

 She dresses to his liking
  What she likes does not really matter
  She styles her hair to his liking
 What she likes does not really matter
  She lets him choose her perfume
  And is so very delighted
 No matter how unpleasant the scent!

A proper wife
 Quickly forgets "the books"
 And the school that taught her about those books
 She takes from her husband
All instruction
  And also from him
  All judgment!
 She sees the world through his eyes
  And through his eyes, even
  Her own life, her joys and tears!

A proper wife
 Must love her husband
  —My husband Kalifa told me so—
To love him very deeply and bless him forever
 Find him handsome and clever
  In every way
 Depend on him
  And on him alone
  And wait
   Blissfully
 For him to bring her life
 And the world!"

J'ai entre les mains
      Ce code pour le moins curieux
      Et n'ose rien en dire
      De peur d'irriter Kalifa . . .

So I have in my hands
    This rather curious rulebook
    And dare not say anything about it
    For fear I will irritate Kalifa . . .

Jubilation

Le Bon Dieu m'a faite femme
Plume de soie berce vie
Piquantes îles évasion ivresse
Femme mandarine, femme jus de fruits
Femme une larme femme une moue
Et savane, et printemps et bambou et couleurs
Se taisent en un hymne unique
Quand cent feux fluides mille lumières
Baignent le monde à miracle les chœurs.

Femme ! Rien. Mais Femme, le Bon Dieu m'a faite tout
Luciole des volcans rosier infernal
Mélodie dans la nuit du promeneur
Femme aveux des sérénades d'anges
Femme feu d'artifice
Femme biche du prestige viril
Femme espérance des enfants
Femme ordre du temps
Et savane, et printemps et bambou et couleurs
Se scellent en un ciel de paix dans mon âme
Goûtant aux spasmes voluptueux
Que mon cœur, ô grâce, muet de plénitude
Dans le secret des joies sans borne, adore.

MARIE CLAIRE DATI (CAMEROON)

*Dati was born in 1955 in Edea, Cameroon, and attended local
schools. She graduated from Yaoundé University in Cameroon
in 1979 and received a translator's certification from Georgetown
University in Washington, D.C., in 1986. Dati has worked as a
singer and actor, appearing in French-language African films, and
writes fiction and drama as well as poetry. She has published a
play and two books of poetry and currently lives in Addis Ababa,
Ethiopia, where she works as a translator.*

Jubilation

The Good Lord made me a woman
A silken feather soothing life
Spicy islands drunken escape
A tangerine woman, a fruit-juice woman
Woman a tear, woman a pout
And a savannah, and a spring and a bamboo and colors
That fall silent in a single hymn
While a hundred moving fires a thousand lights
Bathe the choruses of the miracle world

Woman! Nothing. But Woman, the Good Lord made me
    everything
Firefly of the volcanoes infernal rosebush
Melody in the night of the wanderer
Avowing angelic serenades woman
Fireworks woman
Woman doe of a virile prestige
Woman hope of children
Woman arranger of time
And a savannah, and a spring and a bamboo and colors
That melt into the peaceful sky of my soul
Tasting of the voluptuous spasms
That my heart, O Grace, speechless with plenitude
Adores in the secret of endless joy.

Je déchire

Je déchire,
Je déchire.

Je déchire la page africaine où
Un œuf d'arc-en-ciel
A chair d'ange,
Et chaud comme le son d'une aube d'harmonies . . .

Je déchire la page africaine où
Un ongle de génie,
Fumé dans la rosée s'évaporant
Et odorant comme le bouquet d'une montagne de miracles . . .

Je déchire la page africaine où
Un œil de soleil
Affairé sous un chaume
Et merveilleux et rare comme l'étourdissement divin . . .

Je déchire la vieille figure africaine où
Naquit ma Grand-mère comme Ecrin
Sur un riche millier de feuilles sceptiques de bananier
Entre l'air enfumé et les cals sentant des peaux de mains . . .

. . . Où ma Grand-mère assise sur ses jambes
Sur un petit creux dans un siège de poussière
Pendant des jours et des nuits, immobile
Déposait la larme rouge de la fécondité.

I Tear Out

I tear out
I tear out

I tear out the page of Africa where
A rainbow egg
With angel flesh
And warm like the sound of a harmonious dawn . . .

I tear out the page of Africa where
A fingernail of a genie
Smoked in evaporating dew
And perfumed like the bouquet from mountains of miracles . . .

I tear out the page of Africa where
An eye of sunshine
Busy beneath a thatched roof
And marvelous and rare like divine giddiness . . .

I tear out the old figure of Africa where
My grandmother was born like a Jewel
On a thousand lush septic leaves from the banana tree
Between the smoked-filled air and the scent of calloused hands . . .

. . . Where my Grandmother squatting on her hips
Over a small hollow in a bed of dust
For days and nights, motionless
Dropped the red tear of fecundity.

L'orange

Je trouve dans une orange
L'or du rayon de soleil
Intense au fond de ton âme
Piquant et gonflant tes veines

Ma bouche dans une orange
Boit la pulpe jeune et fraîche
Dont les baisers font tes lèvres

Au creux de mon corps l'orange
Délicieusement pétille
Et ma gorge s'abandonne
Savourant l'instant qui coule

Qui coule qui coule coule et
Quand l'aurore tous feux point
L'orange expire dans la poubelle
Et moi j'éclate sous ta force.

The Orange

I find inside an orange
The gold from a ray of sun
Piercing to the bottom of your soul
Prickling and puffing your veins

My mouth inside an orange
Drinks the pulp young and fresh
Whose kisses shape your lips

In the hollow of my body the orange
Deliciously sparkles
And my throat surrenders
Savoring the instant that flows

That flows and flows and flows and
When the fiery day breaks
The orange vanishes into the trash
And me I explode with your strength.

L'homme

Quand j'eus l'âge de raison,
Et que la coutume voulut que je me marie,
Mon père me retint un soir

Et me confia ceci :

"Quand tu pourras écouter un homme
T'insulter sans mot dire,
Et sans t'émouvoir,
Viens alors me dire que tu te maries :
L'homme est un être faible
Qui n'admet pas qu'on le lui montre.
Quand il se met en colère,
Ses oreilles s'éloignent
De la bouche qui le raisonne.
Laisse-le dire ce qu'il veut,
Et caresse-le où tu peux.
Quand il se calmera et
Qu'il reviendra dans tes bras,
Serre-le comme ton bien,
Berce-le comme il faut.
Il reconnaît alors en toi la mère.
Et c'est ainsi qu'il se sent homme."

MADELEINE DE LALLÉ (BURKINA FASO)

Madeleine de Lallé Kaboré was born in 1955 in Pissin, a village of the prefecture of Lallé, Burkina Faso. She took her place of origin as a penname. Educated in Burkina Faso, she earned a Diplôme d'Etudes Approfondies degree in linguistics and became a professor at the Teaching Institute of Burkina Faso. She has specialized in language teaching, developing and promoting bilingual programs for the country's primary schools.

Man

When I came of age
And tradition dictated I should marry
My father took me aside one evening

And confided this to me:

"When you can listen to a man
Insult you without saying a word
And without being upset
Then come and tell me you are getting married:
Man is a feeble being
Who cannot admit he is so.
When he becomes angry
His ears withdraw
From the mouth that reasons with him.
Let him say what he wants to say,
And caress him where you can.
When he calms down and
Comes back to your arms
Embrace him as if he is your prize,
Soothe him as best you can
He recognizes the mother in you.
And that makes him feel like a man."

La mort d'un homme

Au soir de sa vie
Mon père me fit mander auprès de lui.
Je revis l'intense douleur
Qui émanait des mots

    Qu'il disait avec lenteur :

"Pleure un homme juste un temps,
Mais ton pays toute ta vie",

    M'a-t-il dit ce soir-là.

"La mort d'un homme,
Pour autant qu'elle fasse de la peine
A ceux qui l'aiment et
A ceux qui ont peur
N'est pas une chose grave.
Mais la mort d'un pays,
Si !
La terre est lourde
D'hommes qui ont vécu
Et se nourrira
D'hommes qui vont mourir,
Mais que s'éloigne de nous
L'horrible spectre
D'un pays qui se meurt !"

    Ce soir-la, mon père m'a dit :

"Pleure un homme juste un temps,
Mais ton pays toute ta vie.
Un homme meurt pour son nom,
Pour que son nom puisse
Eclairer la nuit des temps.
Il meurt pour son enfant,
Pour que celui-ci puisse
Perpétuer son nom.
Un homme meurt pour son pays,
Pour que son pays lui survive.

The Death of a Man

At the close of his life
My father had me brought to him.
I recall the intense pain
That came with the words

He slowly spoke:

"Mourn a man for a proper time,
But mourn your country your whole life,"

He said to me that evening.

"The death of a man,
As much as it gives pain
To those who love him and
To those who are afraid
Is not a serious matter.
But the death of a country,
Yes!
The earth is heavy
With men who once lived
And will be nourished
With men who will yet die,
But may the horrible specter
Of a dying country
Never come to us!"

That evening my father said to me:

"Mourn a man for a proper time,
But mourn your country your whole life.
A man dies for his name,
So that his name can
Illuminate the dark times.
He dies for his children,
So that they may
Perpetuate his name.
A man dies for his country
So that it may survive him,

Car à quoi aurait-il servi
D'avoir vécu,
Si sa mort devait entraîner
La mort de son pays ?"

    Ce soir-là mon père m'a dit :

"Pleure un homme juste un temps,
Mais ton pays toute ta vie.
La mort d'un homme
N'est pas chose grave,
La mort d'un pays,
Si !"

For what purpose would it serve
To have lived,
If his death should lead to
The death of his country?"

That evening my father said to me:

"Mourn a man for a proper time,
But mourn your country your whole life.
The death of a man
Is not a serious matter,
But the death of a country,
Yes!"

L'union

Je suis ouragan, je suis tempête
Je suis furie, je suis socle,
Humus ancestral sur lequel mes rêves germent
Imprégnant ma vie d'une mission sacrée
Je gronde, je tonne, je rugis
Je ronronne, je murmure
Je roule pour la liberté, liberté d'être.

Relever les défis
Dénoncer horreurs humaines
Massacres, affres, agonies
Angoisses, frayeurs, douleurs.

Depuis que cette nuit
Soudain le voile s'est déchiré
Que tous deux on a éclos, on a bourgeonné
On a fusionné, on a éclaté avec la vérité
Etalant notre richesse, notre abondance,
Notre luxuriance intime
Allant jusqu'à l'infinie insolence,
Oubliant nos nuits sombres de torture,
De détresse, de dépression,
De fièvres, pour montrer à la lumière
Du jour que nous sommes un et indivisible.

OUMOU DEMBÉLÉ (MALI)

*Born in 1951 in Ségu, Mali, Dembélé was educated in Mali and
Côte d'Ivoire and then in the United States and France. She
received degrees in French, English, and tourism studies, and works
as a senior adviser in Mali's Ministry of Art and Tourism.*

Union

I am hurricane, I am tempest
I am fury, I am pedestal
Ancestral humus from which my dreams sprout
Impregnating my life with a sacred duty
I growl, I thunder, I roar
I purr, I murmur
I drum for freedom, the freedom to be.

Rise up to challenges
Denounce human atrocities
Massacre, terror, agony,
Distress, fright, pain.

Since that night
Suddenly the veil is torn
So together we opened, we blossomed
We merged we exploded into truth
Spreading our riches, our abundance
Our intimate luxuriance,
Opening onto the infinite insolence
Forgetting our nights dark with torture,
With distress, depression
Fever, in order to show the light
Of day that we are one and indivisible.

Kassacks

A Ousmane mon fils

Tu es homme, ce soir !
Tu es homme, mon fils !
    Par ta chair meurtrie
    Par ton sang versé
    Par ton regard froid
    Par ta cuisse immobile.

Et ta mère se souvient
    De la nuit d'amour
    De ses entrailles déchirées
    De ses gémissements silencieux
    De ses reins écartelés
    Des regards envieux de ses rivales mauvaises
    De la succion gourmande de ta bouche-fleur
    Du gris-gris miraculeux qui
    —Avec l'aide d'Allah—
    A guidé tes pas jusqu'à ce jour heureux.

Tu es homme, ce soir !
Tu es homme, mon fils !
    Par la lame tranchante
    Par ton sexe éprouvé
    Par ta peur refoulée
    Par la terre des Ancêtres.

ANNETTE MBAYE D'ERNEVILLE (SENEGAL)

The first African francophone woman to publish a book of poetry, d'Erneville was born in 1926 and educated in Senegal. She earned a teaching degree and then spent several years in Paris studying and working. After her return to Dakar in 1959, she began working for the national radio station, and eventually she became program director for Radio Senegal. She also founded and edited Awa *a Senegalese magazine for women. Her book* Poèmes africains *was published in 1965 and reprinted as* Kaddu *in 1966. Annette Mbaye d'Erneville lives in Senegal.*

Kassacks

For Ousmane my son

You're a man, this night!
You're a man, my son!
> By your bruised flesh
> By your spilled blood
> By your cold look
> By your unshaken thighs

And your mother remembers
> The night of love
> Her torn womb
> Her silent moans
> Her aching loins
> The envious looks of her evil rivals
> The greedy suckling of your flower-mouth
> The miraculous gris-gris that
> —With the help of Allah—
> Guided your steps to this happy day.

You're a man, this night!
You're a man, my son!
> By the sharp razor
> By your tested penis
> By the resistance of fear
> By the earth of the Ancestors.

Gawolo !... chante cet homme nouveau.
Jeunes filles aux seins debout
Clamez son nom au vent.
Selbé N'Diaye, fait danser ce petit homme.

Tu es homme, mon fils.
Tu es homme ce soir
Ils sont tous là :
      Ceux de ta lune première
      Ceux que tu nommes pères.
Regarde, regarde-les bien :
Eux seuls sont gardiens de la terre
De la terre qui a bu ton sang.

Nocturne

A Diarra-Saïdou, la nigérienne

Des bords du fleuve noir, un soir elle est venue :
Oh ! Princesse Djerma !
J'entends encore tinter tes bracelets d'argents,
Adjaratou ma très douce ; chantes-tu toujours
La plainte de la fille offerte au Dieu-Serpent ?
Ce soir-là ton chant disait l'amour, disait la mort !
Ta voix a-t-elle encore les accents de la guitare monocorde
Qui dans le pays de sable rythme les contes d'amour ?
Sais-tu encore les psalmodies nocturnes
Qui font descendre la lune et la transforme en femme ?

Peur me fait esclave !
Les fausses nuits de la cité
Cachent la lune aux yeux tout neufs
Et les Djins au regard bleu
Volent les voix qui chantent le souvenir !

*Gawolo** . . . sing of this new man.
Young girls with firm breasts
Shout his name to the wind
Selbé N'Diaye, make this little man dance.

You're a man my son!
You're a man this night!
They are all here:
> Those of your first moon
> Those you call father.
Look, look at them well:
They are the guardians of the earth
Of the earth that has drunk your blood.

NOTE: *Kassacks are songs of circumcision.*—AUTHOR'S NOTE
Genealogist griot and singer.—AUTHOR'S NOTE

Nocturne

For Diarra-Saïdou, the woman from Niger

> From the banks of the black river, she came one evening
> Oh! Djerma Princess!
> I still hear your silver bracelets jingling
> Adjaratou my sweetest; do you still sing
> The plaintive song of the girl given to the Snake-God?
> That evening your song told of love, of death!
> Does your voice still have the tones of the one-string guitar
> That in the sand-country gives rhythm to love stories?
> Do you still know the nocturnal chants
> That make the moon come down, and change her into a woman?

> Fear makes me a slave
> False nights in the city
> Hide the moon with brand new eyes
> And the Djinn with blue gazes
> Steal the voices singing of memory!

Indépendance

A Marianine, la militante

Que ne suis-je Diali
Maître de la Kora !
Que ne suis-je diseur
Gardien de mots magiques !

Les rimes sur ton nom
Vibrées sur toutes les cordes
Enivrent déjà le cœur des noirs champions,
Indépendance !

Tu n'es pas le mirage qui guide le chamelier !
Tu n'es pas la "m'bakhousse" de l'enfant qui pleurniche
Tu es la coupe d'argent que soupèse le vainqueur

Les femmes se serrent les reins, et, de leurs lourds pilons,
Rythment la marche sure du pays qui se lève.

Tama, Gortong, Dioundioung
Disent aux quatre vents
Que l'Afrique est debout
Et va vers la lumière.

Independence

For Marianine, the militant

If only I were a Jeli*
Master of the Kora†!
If only I were storyteller
Guardian of magic words!

Rhymes for your name
Vibrating on every string
Already exciting the heart of Black champions
Independence!

You are not the mirage that guides the camel-driver
You are not the "m'bakhousse‡" of the crying child
You are the silver cup the victor lifts up

The women tighten their *pagnes* and, with heavy pestles,
Beat in rhythm the confident march of the country rising

Tama, Gortong, Dioundioung§
Announce to the four winds
That Africa has risen up
And moves toward the light.

A griot guitarist—a kind of troubadour (also spelled diali).—AUTHOR'S NOTE
†*West African musical instrument with twenty-one to twenty-six strings.*—EDITOR'S NOTE
‡*Imaginary thing mothers promise children to calm them down when they are crying.*—AUTHOR'S NOTE
§*Different kinds of drums. The dioundioung is a drum used in the kingdom of Sine and Saloum.*—AUTHOR'S NOTE

Si tel était ton plaisir

Si tel était ton plaisir
Hutus et Tutsis vivraient bras dessus dessous
Si tel était ton plaisir
jamais de leur vie les gens de Palestine n'auraient
livré la guerre de pierres et Jérusalem jamais
ne serait comme bombe à retardement
volcan en instance d'éruption
Mais le monde, Jérusalem serait
Le plus sûr le plus doux le plus abordé des havres
Qu'on ne douterait point que c'est en ce lieu précis
Qu'Allah dressera son trône dans six siècles
pour le jugement ultime des dieux en miniature
que nous sommes.

Si tel était ton plaisir
pour "je ne t'aime pas" il n'y aurait pas de place
pour les haines et les déchirements.
Il n'y aurait place que pour "C'est dommage..."

Si tel était ton plaisir
dans les villes qu'on dit bidons
dans les faubourgs et dans les bourgs borgnes
ne souffleraient que chants doux
des rameurs dont parlait l'Aède.

FATOU BINETOU DIAGNE (SENEGAL)

Fatou Diagne appeared in Anthologie de la jeune poésie
sénégalaise (1999), *an anthology of poems selected from among
open submissions by young Senegalese writers. Neither the editors
of that anthology nor those of this present anthology have been able
to contact her or discover any further biographical information.*

If You Had Your Way

If you had your way
Hutus and Tutsis would be living arm in arm
If you had your way
Never would the people of Palestine
have waged the war of stones and Jerusalem might
never be a time bomb
a volcano waiting to erupt
Instead, the world, Jerusalem would be
the safest, the calmest, the most visited harbor
So no one would doubt that in this exact place
In six centuries, Allah will erect his throne
for the last judgment day of the gods in miniature
that we are.

If you had your way
there would be no place for "I don't love you"
for the hatreds and the heartbreaks
There would only be room for "I'm sorry."

If you had your way
in the towns called shantytowns
on the fringes of towns
there would only be the murmur of the
rowers' sweet song* the poet spoke of

Si tel était ton plaisir
Chats et chiens rivaliseraient d'amour éperdu
grives et loups feraient pareil. Et en ma cervelle,
les parcelles non encore structurées, loties le seraient
pour couvrir et pour couver
les rêves vert bleu et blanc des princesses
du Cayor et du Baol.

Si tel était ton plaisir . . .

If you had your way
Cats and dogs would compete in passionate love
Thrushes and wolves would too. And in my mind,
the empty lots, yet unsurveyed or unplotted
would defend and shield
the green blue and white dreams of the princesses
of Cayor and Baol.

If you had your way . . .

*Allusion to the Senegalese poet Birago Diop and to his poem titled
"Le chant des rameurs" [The rowers' song].—EDITOR'S NOTE

Jigeen Reck Nga

Jigeen reck nga !
Reck ! . . . ô douleur de mon sein, douleur sanglante !
Ndeyssan ! Reck ! . . .

Des lèvres lippues, trop lourdes,
Lâchaient un à un, combien pénibles à mon coeur
De femme offensée, ces mots insensés :
Jigeen reck ! . . .

Et lourd comme du plomb coulant,
Aussi lourd que la morgue qu'affichait ce désarticulé,
Authenticité perdue : toi qui ne sais
D'où tu viens, qui tu es, où tu vas.

Jigeen reck ! . . .
Je suis ta MERE, ô fils de mes entrailles.
En mon sein palpitant, par le fil du nombril,
Je te soufflais les échos du vieux monde.
Ton petit pied curieux
Interrogeait la voûte de ma chair.
Je suis ta MERE, ô fils en pleurs dans cette vallée de larmes,
Où le nectar dans la gourde récompense le vainqueur.
Je te chantais, ô fils ! les vertus des anciens ;
Tu triturais, goulu, mon sein moussu.
Au crépuscule flottant, lorsque jinns et "deumms" méchants,
Gobent tout saignant le cœur des enfants,
Je suis le dos sécurisant qui t'offrait le salut.

NDÈYE COUMBA MBENGUE DIAKHATÉ
(SENEGAL)

Born in 1924, and raised and educated in Rufisque near Dakar,
Senegal, Diakhaté spent her working life as a grammar school
teacher in her place of birth. She was a founder of the Women's
Social Action Group in Rufisque. She died in 2001.

Jigéen Rekk Nga

Jigéen rekk nga!*
Rekk! . . . O my heart's grief, bleeding grief!
Ndeyssaan! Rekk! . . .

Heavy thick lips
spit them out one by one, how hurtful to the heart
of an insulted woman, are these senseless words
Jigéen rekk! . . .

And heavy as sinking lead
Heavy as the arrogance of this immature man
Authenticity is lost: you don't know
where you come from, who you are, where you are going.

Jigéen rekk! . . .
I am your MOTHER, O son of my bowels
In my throbbing breast, by the cord of your navel
I breathed into you the echoes of the old world,
Your curious little foot
probed the arch of my flesh
I am your MOTHER, O son crying in this valley of tears,
Where the gourd's nectar is reward of the conqueror
I sang to you, O son! Of the virtues of the elders;
You mouthed, greedily, my full breast.
In the wavering twilight time of djinn and evil *"ndëmm"*†
bloody, devouring the hearts of children
I am the secure back that keeps you safe.

Jigeen reck ! . . .
O frère ! je suis ta SOEUR jolie,
Du même ventre, après toi sortie.
Mère le disait, le répétait chaque fois ;
Père te grondait, quand tu étais méchant.
Et moi, ta SOEUR jolie, je lavais tes Kaftans pleins de boue,
Tu revenais du marécage où, dans la fange nauséeuse,
Tu pourchassais les crabes gris le soir.
Et, sans rancune aucune, en cachette, je te servais,
Ainsi que tes copains gloutons.

Jigeen reck ! . . .
Je suis l'EPOUSE fidèle,
Fille de ton oncle, mon père au grand nom, et
Frère de ta mère "bajjan"
A toi rivée pour la vie, par le lien double,
Je suis celle qui partage, et pour elle
Prend si peu ; qui tisonne en veillant,
Pour que vive le foyer de sa flamme éternelle.

Griot de ma race

Je suis le griot de ma race :
Poète, troubadour ;
Je chante très haut ma race, mon sang,
Qui clame qui je suis.

Je suis . . . bois d'ébène,
Que ne consume le feu lent du mensonge.
Je suis . . . la latérite rouge du sang farouche de mes ancêtres.
Je suis . . . la brousse inviolée,
Royaume des singes hurleurs.

Jigéen rekk! . . .
O brother, I am your pretty SISTER
Following you from the same womb,
Mother said so, repeated it many times;
Father scolded you, when you were bad
And me, your pretty sister, I washed your muddy Caftans,
When you returned from the swamp where
You chased grey crabs in the evening in nauseating muck
And in secret, without rancor, I gave food to you
and to your gluttonous friends.

Jigéen rekk! . . .
I am the loyal WIFE,
Daughter of your uncle, my father in name, and
Brother of your mother, *bàjjan*‡
Attached to you for life, by this double binding
I am the one who shares, and for herself
Takes little; who prods and tends the fire
So that home is kept alive by an eternal flame.

Wolof for "You are only a woman."—AUTHOR'S NOTE
†*Witches.*—AUTHOR'S NOTE
‡*Paternal aunt.*—AUTHOR'S NOTE

Griot of My Race

I am the griot of my race
Poet, troubadour
I loudly sing of my race, my blood
That proclaims who I am

I am . . . ebony wood
Not consumed by the slow fire of lies
I am . . . the red laterite of the fierce blood of my ancestors.
I am . . . the virgin wilderness
The kingdom of howling monkeys

Pas le Nègre des bas quartiers,
Relégué dans la fange fétide, la suie qui colle ;
Là-bas, dans la ville grise, qui accable, qui tue.

Je suis . . . qui tu ignores :
Soleil sans leurre; pas le néon hypocrite.
Je suis . . . le clair de lune serein, complice des ébats nocturnes
Je suis le sang qui galope, se cabre d'impatience
Dans le dédale de mes artères.
Je suis qui tu ignores.
Je crache sur l'esprit immonde.

Et voici que je romps les chaînes,
Et le silence menteur
Que tu jetas sur moi.

Saisons de la vie

Elle allait ce matin, on eût dit qu'elle volait;
Son boubou de mousseline lui faisait comme des ailes !
Ses pieds si légers effleuraient le sentier :
Car enfin ce matin elle allait se marier

Elle marchait ce midi d'un pas ferme et pressé ;
Son boubou de coton, de sueur lui collait ;
Les enfants, le ménage, et son homme qui attend :
Pour une mère, une épouse, quel tracas qu'une maison !

Elle partait dans le soir, en pesant sur ses pas;
Son boubou délavé la faisait plus voûtée :
Les soucis, les tortures, et les ans ont passé ;
Les enfants à leur tour, une fois grands, l'ont quittée

Elle veillait dans la nuit, près du feu qui se meurt,
Comme un soir l'avait fait son vieil homme de mari.
Seule au monde ! dans le noir, égrenant son chapelet,
Et les heures qui se suivent, annonçant la dernière.

Not the *Nègre* from troubled neighborhoods
Relegated to fetid mire, the clinging soot
There, in the gray city, that crushes, that kills.

I am . . . the one you ignore
The sunlight without illusion, not the hypocritical neon.
I am . . . the calm moonlight, complicit in nocturnal love games
I am the blood that gallops, rearing with impatience
In the maze of my arteries
I am the one you ignore
I spit on your vile spirit.

And watch how I break the chains
And the lie of silence
That you hurled at me.

Seasons of Life

That morning she stepped out as if she were flying
Her *boubou** of muslin was spread out like wings!
Her feet barely touched the ground:
Because, finally, that morning she was to be married.

At noontime, she was walking steadily, quickly ahead
Her *boubou* of cotton was clinging with sweat
The children, the housework and her husband waited
For a mother, a wife, what turmoil in a house!

In the evening she set off, heavy on her feet
Her faded *boubou* made her look even more stooped.
The worry, the torture, and the years had passed;
Then the grown children had left her.

In the night she kept watch near the dying fire
Like her husband, the old man had done one evening.
Alone in the world! In the night telling her beads
And the hours that follow each other foretelling the end.

Large dress resembling an ample tunic or caftan.—EDITOR'S NOTE

Jeune femme morte

Elle dormait . . . gentille, menue.
On la disait morte ;
Moi non.

Elle dormait . . . sereine, reposée
Enfin soulagée.

Cette naïade si douce
Accusait une moue légère,
Un soupçon de malice,
De vengeance posthume.
Et, muette, elle semblait dire :
Tans pis ! si vous n'avez su me comprendre ;
Si vous n'avez su, parmi vous me retenir.

Je m'en vais . . .
Au royaume des ondines, au lacis bleu-vert des irréelles.
Je m'en vais . . .
Coulante, gracile, fendant les algues caressantes,
Croisant les sirènes luminescentes.

Je m'en vais . . .
Dans la paix des eaux, les voûtes impalpables,
Le crépuscule des grands fonds.
Je m'en vais . . .
Sans retour.

Young Woman Dead

She was sleeping . . . graceful, slender
They said she was dead;
I didn't.

She was sleeping . . . serene, rested
Relieved at last.

This sweet naiad
Had a slight frown
A hint of spite
A posthumous vengefulness.
And, mute, she seemed to say:
Too bad! If you could not understand me
If you did not know how to keep me with you.

I am leaving . . .
For the kingdom of waves, for the blue-green maze of the unreal
I am leaving . . .
Going down, graceful, parting the caressing sea weeds
Meeting luminous sirens

I am leaving . . .
For the peace of the waters, the unreachable vaults,
the twilight of the great ocean depths
I am leaving . . .
I will never return.

Autre fleur

Fleur
Use de ton arme
Et les pierres chuteront
Use de ton charme
Et les abeilles
Autour de toi
Deviendront pierres

Abstinence

Penser . . .
Au rythme des cauris
Sur les feux d'un soir
Le rire macéré des fétiches fascinés
Dans le vestige des ombres
Abandonner . . .
Les caresses charnelles
De tes paumes brûlantes
Au secours de mes délires
dans la frénésie des corps en sursaut
Oublier . . .
Le souvenir de ton regard enflammé
Caressant mon souffle effréné

KOUMANTHIO ZEINAB DIALLO (GUINEA)

*Diallo was born in 1956 in Labé, Guinea, and received a degree
from Gamal Abdel Nasser University in Conakry. Trained as
an agronomist, she has been an activist for the improvement of
rural living conditions in Guinea and a development consultant
for various international organizations. She has also worked as a
journalist and a radio producer, creating a program to broadcast
poetry in the local languages of Guinea, and helped found literary
and women's associations in the country. Besides her poetry in
French and in Pular, Diallo has published novels and stories.*

Another Flower

> Flower
> Use your spear
> And the stones will fall
> Cast your spells
> And all around you
> The bees
> Will turn to stone

Abstinence

> Thinking . . .
> In the rhythm of cowries
> In the evening's fires
> The laughter softened by fascinated fetishes
> In remnants of shadows
> Surrendering . . .
> The carnal caresses
> Of your burning palms
> That save me in my delirium
> In the frenzied trembling of bodies
> Forgetting . . .
> The memory of your desiring look
> Caressing my wild breath

Le rire fascinant de tes yeux
Et la virilité de ton corps éveillé
Pour m'abstenir
Je m'offre à ces douces heures
Ces heures immortelles
Suspendues au souvenir têtu
Des ultimes confidences.

Lune d'Afrique

J'ai rêvé pour toi
Ami
Une belle lune
Belle comme seule peut l'être
La lune de mon village
Là où les filles s'habillent
De leurs robes couleurs de joie
Et dansent au son grêle du tam-tam
Là où il n'y a pas de néons
Pour ternir la clarté magique
De dame lune
Là où il n'y pas d'édifices
Pour obstruer le passage des rayons lumineux
De dame lune
Là où les grillons s'organisent
Dans un concert muet pour saluer
Dame Lune
Là où les montagnes secouées par
Le son mélodieux de la flûte pastorale
S'élancent pour saluer
Dame Lune
Dans ton silence, ô ! ami
Reçois un morceau de ma belle
Lune d'Afrique
Pour briser la nuit qui te hante
Et un coin de mon ciel bleu
Ajouté à la verdure féerique
De ma belle Afrique
Pour illuminer ton cœur sombre
Et éterniser l'espérance.

The fascinating laughter of your eyes
And the virility of your aroused body
In abstinence
I give myself to those sweet hours
Immortal hours
Suspended in an implacable memory
Of ultimate secrets.

African Moon

I have dreamed for you
Friend
A beautiful moon
Beautiful as only the moon
Of my village can be
In my village where girls dress
In clothes the color of joy
And dance to the slender sound of the drum
In my village where no neon
Dulls the magical clarity
Of Lady Moon
In my village where no buildings
Block the passing of the luminous rays
Of Lady Moon
In my village where crickets orchestrate
A mute concert to salute
Lady Moon
In my village where mountains awakened by
The melodious sound of the pastoral flute
Rise to salute
Lady Moon
In your silence, O, friend
Accept a morsel of my beautiful
African Moon
To break up the night that haunts you
And a corner of my blue sky
To add to the enchanting green
Of my beautiful Africa
To brighten your somber heart
To make hope eternal.

A Karim

Je l'ai vu
Moi aussi
Oublié de tous
Je l'ai vu
Sur le macadam
Comptant s'y faire broyer
Et s'y fondre dans le néant
Tout le monde
D'un seul cri :
Il est perdu ! Il est fini !
Bon pour la prison
La prison à vie
Et nous tous, bien portants
A dix, à cent
Nous avons vu en lui le mal en être
Délinquant
Récidiviste
Assassin
Et personne n'a dit :
Un peu d'amour
Un peu de soleil
Une chance de bonheur
Comme tous les enfants de la Terre
Nous l'avons fui en peste mortelle
D'Oran
Pourtant, au clair de lune
Nous avons crié en chœur :
Nous aimons les enfants !
Vive l'année de l'enfant !

CÉCILE-IVELYSE DIAMONÉKA (CONGO)

*Diamonéka was born in 1940 in Kinkala, Congo-Brazzaville, and
educated in local schools, then at the University of Brazzaville.
After early studies in music, she turned to writing poetry and fiction,
publishing a book of poems after moving to Paris. A longtime associate
of UNESCO and a writer and speaker on questions of gender, children,
and family, Diamonéka currently lives in France.*

For Karim

I saw him
Forgotten by everyone
Including me
I saw him
On the highway
Hoping to be crushed into it
And melt into nothingness
Everyone
Cried as one:
He is lost! He is done!
Good for prison
For life in prison
And the rest of us, well-off
By the tens, and hundreds
We had seen in him the essential evil
Delinquent
Habitual criminal
Murderer
And no one said
A little love
A little sunshine
A little chance for happiness
Like all the children on Earth.
We fled from him as from the fatal plague
Of Oran
Still, by the light of the moon
We cried out together
We love children!
Long live the Year of the Child!

Dis-moi...

Si ce que tu as à dire
N'est pas aussi beau que le silence
Alors, tais-toi
Car il n'y a rien de plus beau
Que ta bouche entrouverte
Sur une parole arrêtée

Dis-moi l'indicible
Dis-moi l'innommable
Dis-le moi avec les mots
Qui se fondront dans le vide
Aussitôt prononcés

Dis-moi ce qu'il y a de l'autre côté du miroir
Derrière tes yeux sans tain
Dis-moi ta vie, dis-moi tes rêves
Dis-moi tes peines et tes espoirs aussi
Et je les vivrai avec toi

Dans un monde de silence et de soie crissante
De regards veloutés et de caresses ouatées
A présent, tout a été dit
Ou presque
Alors chuuuuuuuut......

—(07/09/2002)

NAFISSATOU DIA DIOUF (SENEGAL)

Born in 1973 in Senegal, Diouf attended the Université Montaigne in Bordeaux, receiving master's degrees in modern languages and in international commerce. She has published a collection of short stories, a detective novel, and a number of books for children, as well as poetry. She lives in Dakar, where she is a manager of sales and accounting for SONATEL.

Tell Me . . .

If what you have to say
Is not as beautiful as silence
Then, say nothing
Because nothing is more beautiful
Than your mouth half-open
On a hanging word

Tell me the unspeakable
Tell me the unnamable
Tell me with words
That will melt into nothingness
As soon as you speak them

Tell me what is on the other side of the mirror
Behind your eyes without silvering
Tell me your life, tell me your dreams
Tell me your grief and also your hopes
And I will live them with you

In the world of silence and rustling silk
Of velvet gazes and quilted caresses
Now, everything has been said
        Or almost
                So husssssssssh . . . . . .

Mame Sédar

(Oraison pour Senghor)

Senghor est mort
Triste est la rime

La chandelle consumée
A accompli son destin
Et s'en va retrouver serein
L'insouciance du pâtre
Dans les jardins verdoyants
De son royaume d'enfance

Repose en paix, Mame Sédar
Ton âme universelle
Hantera longtemps
Les sentiers nostalgiques de Joal
Où la mémoire des arbres te dira encore
L'épopée de Gnilane Bakhoum
La geste de Diogoye le fier

Senghor est mort
Mais la rime n'est belle
Car trois mots tombent
Fracassants telles des pierres
Sur le marbre lisse de ta tombe
Non ! La rime n'est belle

Mame Sédar,
Tu reviendras d'entre les ancêtres
Illuminer nos chemins obscurs
Du flambeau de tes mots
Tes vers sont à jamais calligraphies
Au grimoire de l'Universel

[...]

Mame Sédar

(Oration for Senghor)

Senghor is dead
The rhyme is sad

The candle consumed
Has accomplished its destiny
And, serene, goes to find again
The careless freedom of a herdsman
In the green pastures
Of his kingdom of childhood*

Rest in peace, Mame† Sédar
Your universal soul
Will be haunting for a long time
The nostalgic paths of Joal
Where the memory in the trees will tell once again
The epic of Gnilane Bakhoum‡
The gest of Diogoye the Proud§

Senghor is dead
But the rhyme is not beautiful
For three words fall
Shattering like stones
On the smooth marble of your tomb
No! The rhyme is not beautiful

Mame Sédar,
You will return from among the ancestors
To light our dark ways
With the torch of your words
Your lines are forever calligraphies
In the magical scripts of the Universal

[...]

Senghor est mort
L'immortel s'en est allé
Rejoindre les pangols en sanglots
Dans leur bois sacré
Aux fragrances d'écorce et de lait
Les cantiques des moines au prieuré
Pleurent l'enfant prodige du Séminaire
Mais moi, le poète
Je reviendrai en héraut
Chanter le héros
Le poète intemporel
Non, la rime n'est pas belle !

[...]

Mais repose en paix, Mame Sédar
Car Senghor est mort
Mais la rime reste reine !

—(10/01/2002)

Senghor is dead
The immortal is gone
To rejoin the sobbing *pangols*‖
In their sacred wood
With fragrances of bark and of milk
The hymns of monks in the priory
Mourn the Seminary's prodigal child
But I, the poet
I will return as a herald
To sing the hero
The timeless poet
No, the rhyme is not beautiful!

[…]

But rest in peace, Mame Sédar
Because Senghor is dead
But the rhyme remains queen!

"Royaume d'enfance" or "kingdom of childhood" is a phrase coined by
Léopold Sédar Senghor to speak of his childhood and the positive impact it
had on the rest of his social, artistic and political life.
†*Mame is an honorific term for grandparents or ancestors in Wolof.*
‡*Gnilane Bakhoum is Senghor's mother's name.*
§*Basile Diogoye is Senghor's father's name.*
‖*In Serer, Senghor's language, a* pangol *is a spirit of the dead who inhabits*
the land of the living.

Femme

Il paraît que je suis un être essoufflant
    Moi ! Femme
Il paraît que je dois être obéissante
    Moi ! Femme
Il paraît que je suis l'angoisse et la peur
    Moi ! Femme
Cependant, je suis la reine mère
Créatrice des grands hommes
Source de régénération
Depuis ma plus tendre jeunesse
    jusqu'à ma vieillesse
Et au-delà de ma mort
Femmes du monde
    Soyez bénies

RAMATOULAYE DIOUF (SENEGAL)

Ramatoulaye Diouf's work appeared in an anthology of poems selected from among open submissions by young Senegalese writers. Neither the editors of that anthology nor those of this present anthology have been able to contact her or discover any further biographical information.

Woman

They say I'm someone who is tiresome
    Me! Woman
They say I'm someone who must be obedient
    Me! Woman
They say I am anxiety and fear
    Me! Woman
Nevertheless I am the queen mother
Creator of great men
Source of regeneration
From my tenderest youth
    to my old age
And even after death
Women of the world
    Blessings on you.

Terre blessée

Laisse-moi prier
De toutes les forces de mon être
De mon cœur de mon sang
Pour les pays du Sahel

Six millions de Nomades avancent
Rongés de famine jusqu'aux entrailles.
Vingt millions de bêtes meuglent
De faim de soif
Fouillent la terre
Les squelettes des côtes collées à la peau
L'herbe rare qui s'envole
Emporte leur plainte
Au vent passager
Et ils demandent où
Va le torrent de leur destin
Va-t-on les laisser mourir de faim?

Inexistants misérables de misères
Ils ressemblent aux pierres dures
Secs sans vie
Pesants et lourds
Dans leur démarche de désespoir
Ils implorent comme suprême bonheur la mort
Tout le long du Sahara
De l'Afrique à l'Asie

KINÉ KIRIMA FALL (SENEGAL)

Born in Rufisque, Senegal, Fall attended primary school there but did not pursue any other formal schooling. She has published two books of poetry.

Wounded Land

> Let me pray
> With all the strength of my being
> Of my heart of my blood
> For the countries of the Sahel
>
> Six million nomads are moving
> Gnawed to their entrails with famine.
> Twenty million beasts groan
> From hunger from thirst
> Scouring the land
> Skeletal ribs sticking to their skin
> The scarce grass blows away
> Carrying their cries
> To the passing wind
> And they ask where
> The flood of their destiny is going
> Will they be allowed to die of hunger?
>
> The miseries of the miserable do not exist
> They resemble hard stones
> Dry, lifeless
> Burdened and heavy
> With their hopeless gait
> They beg for death as a supreme gift
> The entire length of the Sahara
> From Africa to Asia

Et
Impuissante je ne puis effacer
Chaque pleur
Chaque douleur
Chaque plainte
Impuissante je suis

Dans leur vie sans vie
J'implore comme suprême bonheur
O ma Gloire
Dans ces aubes futures où rampent
Des rayons de jours
Des murmures de l'eau qui tombe
Efface la fêlure de leurs sanglots
Inonde et mouille cette terre
Efface sur leur visage au regard perdu
Cette intense douleur
De ceux qui ne demandent plus rien

Après ces jours de misère
Nombreux comme les palmes
Fais, ô ma Gloire
De leurs nuits sans espérance sans joie
Qu'ils connaissent le bonheur et rayonnent
Comme l'éclat du Soleil de midi

O que l'eau soit !
Que du ciel descende
La grâce des pluies
Que jaillissent puits sources et fontaines
Que boive celui qui a soif
Mange celui qui a faim
Que verdisse et fleurisse
Toute ma terre blessée

O Seigneur
Nos cris
N'éveillent-ils plus
L'écho de Ta miséricorde
De Ta pitié
Pitié Seigneur
Pitié pour ma terre.

And
Powerless, I cannot remove
A single tear
A single pain
A single groan
I am powerless

Into their lifeless life
I ask as a supreme favor
O my Glory
Into these future dawns where
Rays of daylight creep in
The murmurs of falling water
Remove the break in their sobs
Inundate and water this land
Wipe from their distraught faces
This intense pain
Of those who ask nothing more

After these days of misery
As many as the palm trees
Act, O my Glory
Against their nights, without hope, without joy
That they might know happiness and radiance
Like the brightness of the Sun at noon

O let there be water!
Falling from the sky
The blessing of the rains
That gush from wells, springs and fountains
So that the thirsty may drink
That the hungry may eat
That all of my wounded land
Become green and flowery

O Lord
Our cries
No longer awaken
The echo of your Mercy
Of your Pity
Have Pity Lord
Pity for my land.

Prends libre essor
O ma terre
Par delà le Cosmos l'Univers
Mille bienfaits
O ma Gloire
Je te l'implore avec l'énergie du désespoir
A l'Afrique à l'Asie.

Pour Dieu des roses et du parfum

Je convierai toutes les roses
Les essences et les parfums
Demain dans ma demeure
Je mettrai toutes mes parures
Mes plus beaux habits
Et je prierai mon Dieu

Pour que leurs parfums
Cueillent dans mon cœur mon âme
Mon amour de Vous
Et l'emportent à Vous
Par delà les airs
Par delà mon cœur mon âme
Il y a ma vie
Mais par delà ma vie
Il y a mon amour de Vous
Plus grand que ma vie

Hors de moi jaillit pour vous toujours
Une berceuse que vous chante mon cœur
Des cordes du plus profond de Lui
Se tendent comme un arc vers Vous
Vous dit et vous redit toujours
Je vous aime et vous adore Seigneur
C'est un chant que vous chante mon cœur
Inlassablement
Cette mélodie finira en moi
Quand finira ma vie
Si mon chant vous plaît Seigneur
Gardez-moi sous votre sein toujours

Lift yourself free
O my land
Beyond the Cosmos Universe
A thousand good deeds
O my Glory
I beg you with the energy of despair
For Africa for Asia

For God of Roses and Perfumes

I will invite all of the roses,
The oils and perfumes
Tomorrow, in my house
I will wear all of my adornments
My most beautiful clothes
And I will pray to my God

So that these perfumes
Gather within my heart my soul
My love of You
And are brought to You
Beyond the wind
Beyond my heart, my soul
My life is there
But beyond my life
Is my love for You
Far greater than my life

Out of me always pours for You
A lullaby my heart sings to You
Strings deep within Him
Brace like an arch towards You
Telling you again and again
I love you and I adore you Lord
This is a song my heart sings to you
Tirelessly
This melody will end in me
When my life ends
If my song pleases you Lord
Hold me near your heart always

Je vous l'implore
Eveillez-moi de votre amour tous les jours
J'ai faim de votre tendresse toujours
Les mots se perdent dans moi
Je vous aime et je vous adore Seigneur
Cette mélodie me berce
Et me fait fondre de joie
Selon vote amour consolez-moi Seigneur
Sinon je me sens perdue

I beg you
Wake me with your love everyday
I hunger always for your tenderness
The words are lost in me
I love you and I adore you Lord
This melody calms me
And fills me with joy
Console me Lord with your love
Or else I am lost

Merci d'être femme

Merci d'être femme,
D'avoir été enfantée
Pour connaître les douleurs de l'enfantement;
D'avoir tété le sein de ma mère
Pour connaître la joie et le bonheur d'offrir mon lait;
D'avoir été portée au dos
Pour apprendre à élargir mon dos;
D'avoir connu la tendresse de ce cœur maternel
Pour apprendre à acquérir un cœur d'enfant.

Merci d'être femme,
D'être à l'école de la prudence,
De l'endurance et de la patience
Afin de devenir gardienne du foyer,
Pour assurer la protection et l'épanouissement;
D'être un nid de pensées limpides et fécondes,
D'être la terre qui accueille, pour germer,
        Les grains du futur.

Merci d'être femme,
D'être beauté et douceur,
D'être lumière et chaleur,
D'être réserve et amour
Et enfin, mieux que tout cela,
D'être née pour donner,
Donner ma Paix pour la Paix
DE L'HUMANITE.

JÉMIMA FIADJOE-PRINCE AGBODJAN
(TOGO)

Born in 1950 in Batié, Burkina Faso, Fiadjoe-Prince Agbodjan
studied medicine at the University of Dakar and then in France at
the University of Lille. She works as a pediatrician in Lomé, Togo.

Thank You for Being a Woman

Thank you for being a woman
For having been born
To know the pain of childbirth;
For having nursed my mother's breast
To know the joy and happiness of offering my milk;
For having been carried on her back
To learn how to strengthen my back
For having known the tenderness of this maternal heart
To learn how to have a child's heart.

Thank you for being a woman
For being at the school of prudence
Of endurance and of patience
In order to become guardian of the hearth
To insure its protection and fulfillment;
For being a nest of clear and creative thoughts
For being the welcoming earth where grow
        The seeds of the future

Thank you for being a woman
For being beauty and softness
For being light and warmth
For being discretion and love
And finally, more than anything,
For being born to give,
To give my Peace for the Peace
OF HUMANITY.

Hymne à mon pays

A mon père et à ma mère
A mon pays

Dis-moi
Histoire de mon peuple
Tes racines profondes
Lumière en mouvement des hiers conquis
Dis-moi
Les temps fertiles
De l'ensemencement
Les crépuscules éclatés
En palabres fécondes
Dis-moi Histoire
Ton nom

Dis-moi
Ton audace
La clarté singulière de ta marche militante
Sur les chemins arides
De la liberté
Mais dis-moi tous ces hommes
Ces femmes
Qui de leurs mains empreintes
Des promesses de la nature
Ont pétri d'argile rouge
Et de sang

COLETTE HOUÉTO (BENIN)

Born in 1939 in Porto-Novo, Houéto was educated there and then attended university in France, at Strasbourg and Aix-en-Provence. Majoring in German, she taught languages in Benin before going to work at the National Institute of Educational Research, the African Bank for Development in Abidjan, and as an administrator of educational programs for UNICEF in Burkina Faso. She was most recently the Minister of Education in Benin.

Hymn for My Country

For my father and my mother
    For my country

        Tell me
        History of my people
        Of your deep roots
        The moving light of conquered yesterdays
        Tell me
        Of the fruitful times
        Of the sowing
        The twilights flaring
        In fertile talk
        Tell me History
        Your name

        Tell me
        Of your boldness
        The singular splendor of your militant march
        Over the arid paths
        Of freedom
        But tell me also of all these men
        These women
        Whose hands imprinted
        With nature's promise
        Have molded from red clay
        And blood

Cette terre vivante de lumière
Et de sons
Dis-moi le courage et la bravoure de tes guerriers
Devant l'appétit séculaire et vorace
De ces charognards
Ennemis de la libération
Dis-moi tes chants
Et tes cris
Et les codes secrets des tam-tams d'initiation
Dis-moi peuple
Les prières des ancêtres

Sur les assins du devoir
Dis-moi les traces indélébiles
De ces alphabets silencieux
Sur les flancs de tes collines altières
Dis-moi la sérénité de l'initié au corps refait
Par l'onguent de la sagesse
Dis-moi hier
Mais dis-moi aujourd'hui
Dis-moi tous ces humiliés, ces éclopés et ces damnés
Qui chaque jour
Arrachent

Aux chiens bourreaux
Des esclaves modernes
Leur dignité
Dis-moi la clairvoyance mûre
Et l'espérance multiple
Des parias de la terre
Jadis écartés de la table des princes repus
Et qui reviennent aujourd'hui
Fils et seigneurs
De cette terre promise
A la liberté

This earth alive with light
And sounds.
Tell me of the courage and bravery of your warriors
Facing the ancient ravenous hunger
Of those vultures
Enemies of liberation
Tell me your songs
And your cries
And the secret codes of the drums of initiation
Tell me my people
The ancestor's prayers

On the *assin*,* the altars of obligation
Tell me of the ineffaceable marks
Of those silent alphabets
On the sides of your imposing hills
Tell me of the initiate's serenity with their body healed
By the salve of wisdom
Tell me of yesterday
But tell me of today
Tell me of the humiliated, the maimed, and the damned
Who every day
Tear away

Their dignity
From the murdering dogs
Of new slaves
Tell me of the maturing vision
And the many hopes
Of those wretched of the earth
Once pushed away from the table of fat princes
And who today return
Children and rulers
Of this land promised
To freedom

Traditional ancestors' altars in Benin.—AUTHOR'S NOTE

Dites-nous, femmes

(A toutes les races de femmes)

Silence inexprimable,
Parole indéchiffrable
De toutes ces femmes
Un jour rencontrées au confluent
Du partage.

Dites-nous femmes
Qui savez
L'eau l'air et le vent
Les cœurs mis à nu
Pour vous qui voulez
La flamme d'une chandelle
Pourquoi l'espace et le repos
N'ont pas le même goût
Sur les sentiers de votre corps
Dites-nous vous qui donnez
L'origine et la faim
Le plaisir et l'essence
Pourquoi nos libertés
Enfantent la nuit

Et voici que le silence longtemps aliéné
Prend la parole au nom du manifeste
De toutes les femmes
Debout

Women, Tell Us

(For women of all races)

Unspeakable silence
Incomprehensible speech
From all these women
Meeting one day at the confluence
Of our commonality.

Women, tell us
You who know
The water, the air and the wind
The naked hearts
For you who desire
The flame of a candle.
Why space and repose
Don't have the same feeling
In the pathways of your bodies.
Tell us, you who give
The beginning and the longing
The pleasure and the essence
Why from our freedoms
The night is born

And here it is that the silence alienated for so long
Seizes speech in the name of a manifesto
Of all women
Rising

Pourquoi pourquoi demandez-vous
Hommes des paradis artificiels
Et bien écoutez donc
Une dernière fois
Semblables aux parias
De la terre
Nos cœurs gorgés de vos trahisons
Exaspérés du bel immonde
De vos "je t'aime" fugitifs
Las des architectures sournoises
De vos discours en miettes
Viennent au point du jour maintenant
Proposer un nouveau pacte

Soyons les artisans de Renaissance
De Co-naissance
Et de Reconnaissance
Ensemble aujourd'hui
Saluons d'un même regard mouillé
La danse parfumée des fleurs
De nos cactus
Partons
Retrouvons les parcours familiers
De nos rues
De nos champs
De nos trottoirs d'usines
Echangeons nos mains nos pensées
Nos doutes nos intuitions
Et nos désirs assumés
Puis sur les herbes humides
Sous les frondaisons épanouies
Des Caïlcédrats de nos vallées
Apprivoisons le temps
Et recréons l'histoire
De nos œuvres d'avenir
Avec la sève vive de la graine
Et la patience des racines de lumière

Why why do you demand
Artificial paradises, men!
Well then, listen
One last time
Like the wretched
Of the earth
Our hearts are filled with your treason
Exasperated by your beautiful vileness
By your fugitive "I love yous"
Tired of the clever architecture
Of your piecemeal speeches.
We are coming now at dawn
To propose a new pact.

Let us be the artisans of Renaissance
Of new-born Common Knowledge
And of Recognition
Today as one
Let us cheer with our watery eyes
The fragrant dance of
Our cactus flowers
Let us go
Let us find again the familiar ways
Of our streets
Of our fields
Of our factory pavements
Let us intertwine our hands our thoughts
Our doubts our intuitions
And our affirmed desires.
Then on the wet grasses
Beneath the blossoming
Cailcidrat trees of our valleys
Let us reclaim time
And re-create the history
Of our future works
With the living milk of the seed
And the patience of the roots of light.

Agoo peuple d'enfants

(A nos enfants et à tous les enfants du monde)

Agoo petits amis des rues
Des champs
Des cours des écoles et des villages
Agoo peuples d'enfants
Qui explorez les paysages familiers
Des quartiers de ville et de campagne
Agoo pour vos espaces vivants
Agoo pour vos espaces vibrants
Vos espaces de danses et de chants
Agoo   Agoo   Agoo
Ouvrez-nous vos territoires de liberté
Accueillez-nous de vos cris de joie et d'espoir
Laissez-nous sécher vos larmes
Que brillent vos regards que sonnent vos rires
Venez accourez faisons des rondes ensemble
Echangeons nos pensées et vos secrets
Apprivoisons le temps
Pour mieux entendre parler
Ecouter
L'enfance qui vous habite
Différente
Irréductible
Agoo vous bâtisseurs de l'avenir
L'avenir dans le grand sourire

De l'aube
Sur les cactus

Agoh-o, the Children's Nation

(For our children and all the children of the world)

Agoh-o little friends of the streets
Of the fields
Of the schoolyards and villages
Agoh-o nation of children
Exploring the familiar landscapes
In the neighborhoods of town and village
Agoh-o for your living spaces
Agoh-o for your vibrant spaces
Your spaces of dances and songs
Agoh-o   Agoh-o   Agoh-o
Open your lands of liberty to us
Welcome us with your cries of joy and hope
Let's dry your tears
Let your eyes shine and your laughter resound
Come, hurry, let's do a circle dance
Let's exchange our thoughts, your secrets
Let's suspend time
To hear your talk better
To listen
To the child living in you
Unique
Irreducible
Agoh-o builders of the future
A future with the huge smile

Of dawn
Above the cactus

NOTE: Agoh-o *is an expression of the Fon language spoken in Benin. It is mostly used when, in a crowd, one has to ask for space to get through. In this context, the narrator uses the term* Agoh-o *as a means of announcing her presence and asking permission to enter the special world of children.*

Fermée pour inventaire

Il n'y a rien à vendre aujourd'hui
Ni sourire
Ni mot doux
Ni mot aigre
Ni mot aigre-doux
Je suis fermée
Fermée pour inventaire

Je n'achète rien aujourd'hui
Ni fou rire
Ni échange de propos doux
Ni échange de propos aigres
Ni échange de propos aigre-doux
Je suis fermée
Fermée pour inventaire

Toute la boutique sera visitée aujourd'hui
Les rayons vides
Les rayons pleins
Les rayons à moitié vides
Les rayons à moitié pleins
Tout sera épousseté
Tout sera vu
Tout sera revu
Tout sera compté

MONIQUE ILBOUDO (BURKINA FASO)

*Born in 1959 in the capital, Ouagadougou, Ilboudo attended the
university there, earning a doctoral law degree and teaching in
the law school. Besides her poetry she has written on gender issues
and published two novels, one of which,* Le mal de peau, *won
the Grand prix imprimerie nationale du meilleur roman. The
second,* Murekatete, *was a product of the FestAfrica project to
memorialize the Rwandan genocide. Ilboudo has served in various
capacities for the government of Burkina Faso, notably as Secretary
of State for Human Rights.*

Closed for Inventory

> There is nothing to sell today
> No smile
> No sweet word
> No sour word
> No sweet and sour word
> I am closed
> Closed for inventory
>
> I am not buying anything today
> No crazy laugh
> No sweet talk
> No sour talk
> No sweet and sour talk
> I am closed
> Closed for inventory
>
> The entire store will be inspected today
> The empty shelves
> The full shelves
> The half-empty shelves
> The half-full shelves
> Everything will be dusted
> Everything will be checked
> Everything will be rechecked
> Everything will be counted

Sur une balance tout sera pesé
Rien ne sera lésé
Sur le plateau gauche l'actif
Sur le plateau droit le passif

Demain si tout n'est pas à prendre
S'il reste de l'énergie à vendre
Si elle retrouve son bien-être
La boutique rouvrira peut-être
Mais aujourd'hui il n'y a rien à vendre
Rien à acheter rien à prendre
Je suis fermée
Fermée pour inventaire.

Je souffre

Je souffre
Du manque de moyens
Des P.A.S.
Qui passent et repassent
De la dévaluation
Qui m'humilie
Du F.M.I.
Qui m'écrase
Du système de valeurs
Qui m'exclut
De la pensée unique
Qui m'étouffe

Je souffre
De l'aide
Généreuse ou déguisée
De la pitié
Feinte ou sincère
De l'arrogance
Méchante ou risible

Everything will be weighed on a scale
Nothing will be ignored
On the left tray the assets
On the right tray the liabilities

Tomorrow if everything isn't up for grabs
If some energy is left for selling
If she finds her wholeness again
The store will open again, maybe
But today there is nothing for sale
Nothing to buy, nothing to grab
I am closed
Closed for inventory.

I Suffer

I suffer
From a lack of means
From S.A.P.*
That come and go
From the devaluation
That humiliates me
From the I.M.F.†
That crushes me
From a value system
That excludes me
From the single-mindedness
That smothers me.

I suffer
From the aid
Generous or disguised
From the pity
Feigned or sincere
From the arrogance
Malicious or mocking

Je souffre
Du regard
Qui me discrimine
Des charters
Qui m'éconduisent

Je souffre
D'être un dépotoir
De manger les restes
De vêtir les hardes
De penser les pensées
Des Autres

Je souffre
Et ne suis pas fière
De mon impuissance.

—*LLN le 24 octobre 1996*

I suffer
From the look
That discriminates against me
From chartered flights
That turn me away

I suffer
From being a dumping ground
From eating leftovers
From dressing in rags
From thinking the thoughts
Of Others

I suffer
And I am not proud
Of my powerlessness.

*Structural Adjustment Programs
†International Monetary Fund

Les jupes

J'aime pas les jupes
Ni les courtes
Ni les longues
Ni les droites
Ni les plissées

J'aime pas les jupes
Les courtes m'exhibent
Les longues m'entravent
Les droites m'étouffent
Les plissées m'encombrent

J'aime pas les jupes
Belles ou laides
Rouges ou vertes
Courtes ou longues
Droites ou plissées

J'aime pas les jupes
Sauf si elles sont culottes
Mais la jupe-longue-plissée
C'est la pire de toutes !
J'aime pas les jupes.

Skirts

I don't like skirts
Not short ones
Not long ones
Not straight ones
Not pleated ones

I don't like skirts
The short ones show me
The long ones slow me
The straight ones smother me
The pleated ones oppress me

I don't like skirts
Pretty or ugly
Red or green
Short or long
Straight or pleated

I don't like skirts
Except if they're culottes
But the long pleated skirt
That's the worst of all!
I don't like skirts.

Extraits de *Les tombes qui pleurent*

Cesse
Tes sanglots
Les morts
Ne pleurent plus.
Je déposerai
Un bouquet de fleurs,
Ni blanches
Ni roses,
Je déposerai sur ta tombe,
Un bouquet
De fleurs noires.
Recueille

Recueille ces larmes
Pour
Souvenir.
Prends,
Prends ce désespoir,
Pour
Espoir.
Entends,
Entends
La plainte de ces vers.
Les âmes grelottent,
Dans des corps angoissés.

[...]

SANDRA PIERRETTE KANZIÉ
(BURKINA FASO)

*Kanzié was born in 1966 in Abidjan. She received her early
education in Abidjan and bordering countries of Côte d'Ivoire.
She attended secondary school at Lycée Mixte Montaigne de
Ouagadougou, where she earned her* baccalauréat *degree in 1988.*

From *The Tombs That Weep*

Cease
Your sobbing.
The dead
No longer cry.
I will place
A bouquet of flowers,
Neither white
Nor pink,
I will place on your grave,
A bouquet
Of black flowers.
Gather

Gather the tears
For
Memory
Take
Take this despair
For
Hope
Hear
Hear
The moaning of these verses
Souls shiver
In anguished bodies

[…]

Pour le voyage
Le voyage
Des éternités
J'irai répondre
A l'appel
A l'appel des aïeux
Pour
Ne plus goûter
A la fraîcheur
Des poisons,
Des vies
Sans vie.

On the voyage
The voyage
Of eternities
I will answer
The call
The call of the ancestors
To
No longer taste
The fresh
poisons
Of lifeless
Lives.

Femme

> Usée
> Fragile
> Terrible
>
> Tu es
> Larme
>
> Tu es
> Mienne
>
> Le monde te fouette de ses lanières de honte
> Il te brise de férocité-lâcheté
> Il t'étrangle de son ignorance
> Il t'abîme de ses sordides sorcelleries
> Armé de flèches métal-dollars
> Il t'avilit te recouvre de sa cuirasse diabolique
>
> Triste
> Tu endures
>
> . . .

MALLAÏ LÉLÈL (NIGER)

Lélèl was born in 1963 in Maibourgourma, Niger, and she received her early education there. She took a baccalaureate in 1982 and a master's degree in modern literature in 1988 from the University of Niamey. She published her first poems in 1995 and has worked as a journalist writing on the social conditions for women and children in Niger. She is currently press attaché for the Niger Ministry of Development.

Woman

Worn out
Fragile
Terrible

You are
A tear

You are
My own

The world whips you with lashes of shame
It breaks you with craven ferocity
It strangles you with its ignorance
It ruins you with sordid sorceries
Armed with arrows of metal-dollars
It debases you with its diabolical armor

Sad
You endure

. . .

Corruption
Cupidité
Mensonge
Tribalisme
Fatalité
Reniement
Cécité
Sénilité
Bassesse
Tourmente
Laideur

. . .

Jamais un reproche
Dans ta voix

Femme
Relève tes yeux baissés
Montre ta gorge ensanglantée
Livides
Tes fils et filles s'acharnent à te dépecer
Tourmentés
Ils te rouent de coups
Ombres effondrées et prostrées
Ils pleurent de te miner

Femme
Eau brûlante
Larme troublante
Allume dans le regard des tiens

Ardeur
Tu es l'Etincelle qui
Incendie
Effluves et Ondes
Prophétise
Douceur

Corruption
Greed
Lies
Tribalism
Fatality
Denial
Blindness
Senility
Baseness
Torment
Ugliness

. . .

Never a reproach
In your voice

Woman
Raise your lowered eyes
Show your bloody throat
Livid
Your sons and daughters implacably cut you to pieces
Tormented
They hit you again and again
Helpless and brazen shadows
They weep as they wear you away

Woman
Burning water
Disturbing tear
Ignite in the gaze of dear ones

Ardor
You are the Spark that
Ignites
Fragrances and Waves
Prophesying
Sweetness

Femme Ruisseau Amour
Tu régénères patiemment les tiens
De leurs souillures

Pénétrés enfin d'Abondance
Ils prient et distillent
Le chant de la confession

Confiants de vérité
Dépositaires des âges
Ils avancent dans
La Sagesse de Ta Lumière

Femme
Motte de Sable
Pubère Afrique

Tu transmets à tes fils et tes filles ton éternité
Les initiant à l'alphabet du Bonheur
Dans le souffle et le secret du silence.

Woman Stream Love
Patiently you cleanse your dear ones
Of defilement

Filled at last with Plenitude
They pray and release
The song of their confession

Confidants of truth
Trustees of time
They move forward in
The Wisdom of Your Light

Woman
Lump of Earth
Pubescent Africa

You pass to your sons and daughters your eternity
Introducing them to the alphabet of Happiness
In the breath and the secret of silence.

Est-ce bête !

Il y a des contours et des lignes élastiques
Il y a des creux et des rebondissements
Des ronds comme des dos d'âne sur les pistes de chantiers
Et il a des cavités comme un jeu de songo.
Il y a la chaleur tiède des coins de feu mourant
Et l'humidité visqueuse des vapeurs de marais.

Il y a du mou comme de l'argile pétrie
Il y a du ferme comme des balles gonflées
Il y a des yeux qui se meurent pour s'exprimer
Des yeux toujours en quête d'une réponse
La réponse d'une question toujours posée
Mille questions aussi vieilles que le monde :

Suis-je belle ?

Il y a une bouche qui remue
Une bouche qui s'ouvre et se referme
Comme huîtres au soleil
Une bouche s'étouffe et expire
Comme baudruche en transes
Une question, encore une question :

Suis-je aimée ?

WEREWERE LIKING (CAMEROON)

Born in 1950 in Bondé, Cameroon, Liking is one of the most prominent African writers of the postcolonial period. She has published prolifically, poetry, novels, plays, art criticism, and political commentary. She has also worked as an actress, director, and choreographer for her own dramatic productions, which have been performed in numerous international venues. Since 1978 Liking has lived in Côte d'Ivoire, where she established the Ki-Yi community of artists.

Isn't This Silly!

There are contours and elastic lines
There are hollows and bends
Curves like bumps on the paths of building sites
Cavities like on a *songo* game board
There is mild warmth at the edges of a dying fire
And the clammy dampness of vapors from the marsh

There is softness like kneaded clay
Stiffness like inflated balls
There are eyes dying to express themselves
Eyes always searching for an answer
The answer to a question always asked
A thousand questions as old as the world:

Am I beautiful?

There is a mouth that moves
A mouth that opens and closes
Like oysters in the sun
A mouth choking and expiring
Like a balloon crazily dancing
A question, yet another question:

Am I loved?

Encore une question
Et voilà des mains qui tremblent
Comme des lianes dans un courant
Voici des doigts qui se crispent
Comme des mille-pattes sous le pétrole

Suis-je utile ?

Voici une question
Et encore une autre
Voici mille questions
Et voici une réponse
Une réponse aussi vieille que le monde

Oui
Est-ce bête une femme !

Pouvoir

Il est des mots comme des baumes
Ils adoucissent et laissent un goût de menthe
Il est des regards comme de la laine d'agneau
Ils enveloppent et réchauffent dans la caresse
Il est des sourires comme des pleines lunes
Ils illuminent avec intimité

Pouvoir !
Pouvoir regarder
Pouvoir déceler
Pouvoir deviner
Pouvoir sentir
Et être heureux !

Il est des promiscuités enivrantes
Et des frôlements comme des caresses de soleil
Furtives et discrètes et excitantes
Elles laissent un goût d'attente !

Yet another question
And here are hands that tremble
Like vines in a stream
And here are fingers that stiffen
Like millipedes in kerosene

Am I useful?

Here is a question
Yet another one
Thousands of questions
And here is an answer
An answer as old as the world.

Yes
Isn't a woman silly!

To Be Able

There are words like a balm
They sweeten and leave a taste of mint
There are gazes like the wool of a lamb
They enfold and warm like a caress
There are smiles like full moons
They enlighten with intimacy

To be able!
Able to look
Able to discover
Able to predict
Able to feel
And be happy!

There are intoxicating promiscuities
And soft touches like caresses of sunlight
Furtive and discrete and exciting
They leave a taste of anticipation!

Pouvoir
Pouvoir sentir
Et être heureux !

Il est des caresses alarmantes
Qui laissent sur le qui-vive !
Il est des noms qui augurent du destin
Et des phrases comme des décrets.

Pouvoir déceler
Pouvoir
Et être heureux !

Il est des visages comme des proverbes
Enigmatiques et symboliques
Ils appellent à la sagesse
Parce que la vie c'est l'avenir
Et que l'avenir c'est toi

Ah pouvoir
Pouvoir deviner
Et être heureux !

Il est des beautés merveilleuses
Présentes et nombreuses là
Sur le nez là sous nos yeux

Pouvoir
Ah pouvoir regarder
Oui pouvoir voir
Car voir c'est comprendre
Que l'amour
Que le bonheur
C'est aussi vrai
Et aussi près
Que tu es là.

To be able
Able to feel
And be happy!

There are alarming caresses
That leave one on guard
And there are names that foretell fate
And phrases like decrees.

To be able to discover
To be able
And be happy!

There are faces like proverbs
Enigmatic and symbolic
They call up wisdom
Because life is the future
And the future is you

Ah, to be able
Able to predict
And be happy!

There are marvelous beauties
Present and numerous there
Under the nose there before our eyes

To be able
Ah, able to look
Yes, able to see
Because to see is to understand
That love
That happiness
Is as true
And as near
As your being here.

Extraits de *Orphée-Dafric*

Je l'aime
Je l'aime comme on ne peut aimer que soi-même
Son souffle est comme la brise du soir.
La salive de sa bouche est un miel des forêts vierges
Savoureux et odoriférant à enivrer
Sa peau est velours de soie
Je l'aime

[...]

Où es-tu Nyango ?
Réponds-moi mon amour !
Je t'aime
Je t'aime comme on ne peut aimer que l'image de Dieu
Ton regard ouvre sur des mondes inconnus
Et je découvre les merveilles de la création
Je me sens grandir, je m'étends, je m'élargis
Et je découvre Dieu en moi
Et je l'aime ... Et je t'aime
Et je m'aime en toi.

Extraits de *Elle sera de jaspe et de corail*

Il lui parle du plaisir ...
Ah le plaisir dans tous les sens et à tous les niveaux

[...]

La beauté d'une perle d'eau
D'un reflet d'or sur une peau noire
L'éclat moiré d'un velours de soie
L'ondulation frisée de poils en soies sur une peau lisse
La brise du soir dans les cheveux
La fraîcheur d'une goutte de rosée sur la joue
La vraie valeur d'un contact de peau
D'une caresse ...

From *Orphée-Dafric*

I love her
I love her like one can only love oneself
Her breath is like the evening breeze
The saliva of her mouth is honey from virgin forests
Savory and perfuming it intoxicates
Her skin is watered silk
I love her

[...]

Where are you Nyango?
Answer me my love!
I love you
I love you as one can only love God's image
Your gaze opens onto worlds unknown
And I discover the marvels of creation
I feel myself grow, I reach out, I become more
And I discover God in me
And I love him ... And I love you
And I love myself in you.

From *It Shall Be of Jasper and Coral*

He speaks to her of pleasure ...
Ahh, pleasure in every sense and at every level

[...]

The beauty of a bead of water
Of a gold sheen on Black skin
The shimmering patterns of watered silk
The curling undulations of silky hair on smooth skin
The evening breeze in your hair
The coolness of a drop of dew on your cheek
The true measure of touching your skin
of a caress ...

Extraits de *L'amour-cent-vies*

Cesse de pleurer je te raconte le mystère du mâle :
Il est myriade d'atomes éléments épars
Il est poussière et grains de sable
Pour être forme force
Pour devenir volume figure rocher marbre
Il faut la femme
Le liant consolideur créateur
Dieu est femme et la femme le sait
Et la femme le tait
Dieu sait pourquoi . . .
Voici pourquoi l'homme a peur de la femme
Et tient tant à la première place sur la terre . . .

Prête-moi ton corps

Il lui avait dit :
Prête-moi ton corps, mère de la vie
Comme une couverture, un bouclier
Contre le froid de ma solitude
Contre ma fragilité, ma timidité
Contre la peur qui me freine l'activité

Prête-moi ton corps, femme de ma vie
Ton corps comme un socle, un habit
Et je poserai mes actes dans la vie
Comme au creux de tes reins ma semence
Mes actes pour toi, comme une belle danse

Prête-moi ton corps avec ton cœur qui m'enflamme
Ton cœur qui m'implique, qui en appelle à mon âme
Ne le nie pas, je ne dors plus des cris de ton silence
Prête-moi ton corps qui marche comme on danse
Dis-moi oui, et que la vie nous devienne une cadence

From *Love-across-a-Hundred-Lives*

> Stop crying I'll tell you the mystery of the male:
> He is a myriad of scattered atoms elements
> He is dust and grains of sand
> To take on shape and strength
> To become mass form rock marble
> A woman is needed
> The mediating creative link.
> God is woman and woman knows it
> And woman keeps this secret
> God knows why . . .
> This is why man fears woman
> And holds so tightly to the very first place on earth . . .

Lend Me Your Body

> He said to her:
> Lend me your body, mother of life
> Let it be a covering, a shield
> Against the coldness of my solitude
> Against my fragility, my timidity
> Against the fear that slows my action
>
> Lend me your body, woman of my life
> Your body like a pedestal, like a costume
> And I will perform my acts in life
> Like my seed in the space of your loins
> My acts for you, like a beautiful dance
>
> Lend me your body with your heart that inflames me
> Your heart that implicates me, that calls to my soul
> Do not deny it, I can no longer sleep with your cries of silence
> Lend me your body that walks as if dancing
> Say yes, and let life become a rhythm to us

Quand la vie s'éteint

Une vie s'éteint
Une autre renaît
Nous sommes les descendants
De nos morts
Chaque famille conserve les siens
Chaque être conserve sa lignée
Notre sommeil les fait revivre
Ils renaissent chaque nuit en nous
S'habillent de nos guenilles
Se mouvant de nos membres
Marchant souvent dans nos ombres
S'enivrant de nos désirs
Et s'évanouissant en nos réveils.
Quand la vie s'éteint !

Le gros œil du Bon Dieu

J'ai cherché à savoir
D'où venait la lune,
Cette princesse
Couleur d'argent

J'ai voulu comprendre
Où allait la lune,
Cette princesse
Qui illumine le ciel

HORTENSE MAYABA (BENIN)

Mayaba was born in 1959 in Djougou in the north of Benin and attended secondary school in Cotonou. She left government work in order to concentrate on writing, painting, and craft work, and has published poetry, fiction, and children's literature. Her novel L'univers infernal *appeared in 1997. She lives in Benin.*

When Life Ends

A life ends
Another begins
We are the descendents
Of our dead
Each family keeps their own
Every being keeps their lineage
Our sleep makes them live again
In us they are reborn each night
Wearing our tattered clothes
Moving with our limbs
Walking often in our shadows
Drunk with our desires
And vanishing with our waking
When life ends!

The Great Eye of the Good Lord

I tried to find
Where the moon came from,
That princess
The color of silver

I wanted to understand
Where the moon went,
That princess
Who lights up the sky

J'ai tenté de découvrir
Qui commandait à la lune,
Cette princesse
Des nuits d'Afrique

J'ai enfin compris
Ce qu'était la lune,
Cette princesse du ciel
C'est le gros oeil du Bon Dieu

I tried to discover
Who commands the moon,
That princess
Of Africa's nights

At last I understood
What the moon was,
That princess of the sky
She is the great eye of the Good Lord

Martyrs

À ceux qui n'ont pas veécu Thiaroye
Pour Ousmane Sembène

Thiaroye à l'aube !

Dans un grand silence
L'Afrique endeuillée recueille ses fils

Thiaroye à l'aube !
Une aube où l'Afrique a porté sa robe de nuages

Orphelins mossis de Nouna
Bambaras Dogons des grottes de Sanga
Lébous des rivages de Ngor
Orphelins du Levant et du Couchant
Orphelins des bords du Bénin
Orphelins des lagunes
Tournez-la face !

Thiaroye à l'aube !
Le sang pleure d'avoir souillé la terre mère

Thiaroye à l'aube
Quand le sang rouge a giclé sur la peau noire
Le grand baobab a frémi
Ont vagi les crocodiles du Djoliba
Et le sabre du Moro-Naba a sué dans son fourreau.

Thiaroye à l'aube !

MAME SECK MBACKÉ (SENEGAL)

Mbacké was born in 1947 in Gassas, Senegal. She graduated from the Institut des Hautes Etudes Internationales in Paris. A writer in Wolof as well as French, Mbacké has held various diplomatic posts with the Senegalese Foreign Service, including seven years in Paris as the primary liaison for immigrants from Senegal. She has published a novel and a play as well as four volumes of poetry.

Martyrs

To those who lived Thiaroye*
For Ousmane Sembène

      Thiaroye at Dawn!

      In a great silence
      Mourning Africa gathers up her sons

      Thiaroye at Dawn!
      A dawn when Africa wore her robe of clouds

      Mossi Orphans from Nouma
      Dogons Bambara from the Sanga caves
      Lebou from the beaches of Ngor
      Orphans of the Levant and of the West
      Orphans from the shores of Benin
      Orphans of the lagoons
      Avert your eyes

      Thiaroye at Dawn!
      The blood cries for staining mother earth

      Thiaroye at Dawn!
      When red blood spurted on Black skin
      The great baobab trembled
      The crocodiles in the Djoliba wailed
      And the saber of the Moro-Naba sweat in its sheath

      Thiaroye at Dawn!

Les armes ont craché leurs flammes
Les hommes ont craqué
Ces hommes qui
Laissant froide la cendre du foyer
Incultes les champs
S'étaient écriés d'une seule voix
Vive la France !

Aux armes citoyens
Citoyens noirs Tirailleurs d'Outre-Mer
Reposez sous le sceau des baïonnettes

Thiaroye à l'aube !
Et les veuves se sont décoiffées
Pour ne plus regarder
Les médailles gagnées "au champ d'honneur".
Dans les rizières de sang
Sillonnant les routes de ma chair
Cent canons ont tonné
Pour rejoindre la clameur du jazz à l'agonie de l'aube.

Et les fils de Rufisque
Chantent encore ces hommes du grand sommeil.

The weapons have spit their flames
The men have gone mad
These men
Leaving the ashes of the hearth cold
The fields untilled
Cried out in one voice
Vive la France!

To arms citizens!
Black citizens *Tirailleurs* from Outre Mer
Rest beneath the seal of the bayonets.

Thiaroye at Dawn!
And the widows unbraided their hair
To no longer look at
The medals won "on the field of honor."
In the rice fields of blood
Furrowing the tracks of my flesh
One hundred cannons roared
To repeat the clamor of jazz at the agony of dawn.

And the sons of Rufisque
Still sing those men of the Long Sleep.

*A few miles away from Dakar, Thiaroye is a small town
where military barracks were located. On December 1, 1945,
in an organized movement, Senegalese "tirailleurs" or soldiers
demanding the pay they were owed for their military service were
gunned down by local contingents of the French Army.*

J'irai à toi

Rampant à quatre,
J'irai à toi

Roulant en boule,
J'irai à toi.

Raflant les épines,
J'irai à toi.

Au matin de la jeunesse,
Comme à l'aube de la vieillesse
Au crépuscule de la fraîcheur,
Comme à la nuit de la sécheresse
J'irai à toi.

Eprise,
Je viens à toi.

Heureuse,
Je viens à toi.

Espérante,
Je viens à toi

Des abords du désir flamboyant,
Pétillant de roses colorées,
Le sentier de la passion
S'exhibe joyeux.

AMINATA NDIAYE (SENEGAL)

Born in 1974 in Dakar, Ndiaye is a musician as well as a writer.
She studied natural sciences at the University Cheikh Anta Diop.
In 1995 she won the first prize in poetry during the commemoration
of the International Women's Day.

I Will Come to You

> Crawling on all fours
> I will come to you.
>
> Rolled into a ball
> I will come to you.
>
> Covered in thorns
> I will come to you.
>
> In the morning of youth
> In the dawn of old age
> In the dusk of the rainy season
> In the night of the dry season
> I will come to you.
>
> Loving,
> I come to you.
>
> Happy,
> I come to you.
>
> Hoping,
> I come to you.
>
> Next to extravagant desire
> Sparkling with colorful roses
> The path of passion
> In joyous display.

Le Fuyant m'attire,
Je m'embarque.

Entière,
Je suis à toi.

Eprise,
Je suis à toi.

Heureuse,
Je suis à toi.

Plis et replis
De vagues nonchalantes,
L'horizon se moule
En losange auréolé d'or.

Lumière aveuglante
Tes rayons m'ont transpercé l'âme
Le sang coule
Mon cœur saigne.

The ephemeral attracts me,
I embark.

Complete,
I am yours.

Loving,
I am yours.

Happy,
I am yours.

Nonchalant waves
Folding, unfolding
The horizon cast
In a haloed lozenge of gold.

A blinking light
Your rays pierce my soul
The blood flows
My heart bleeds.

Le cheveu

J'ai vu un long cheveu
Près d'une fontaine
Un cheveu qui a conservé
L'éclat d'une vie intense
Il m'a transmis par une caresse
Le message d'une femme
Belle pleine d'envie de vivre
Mais trop tôt disparue
Pour avoir voulu connaître
Le monde des songes
D'où l'on ne revient jamais.

Noyade

Ni cris ni soupirs
Ni pleurs ni lamentations
Ne peuvent l'émouvoir
Il reste insensible
A la souffrance
Du cœur déchiré
Et continue à rouler ses eaux
Oubliant qu'il tient prisonnier
L'enfant
Que la mère attend
Sur la rive.

AMÉLIA NÉNÉ (CONGO)

Néné was born in 1954. She was one of the first Congolese women to publish a literary work. She died in 1996.

The Strand of Hair

I saw a long strand of hair
Beside a spring
A strand which held
The brilliance of an intense life
With a touch it passed to me
The message of a beautiful
Woman filled with the longing to live
Yet she passed away too quickly
For wanting to know
The world of dreams
From which no one ever returns.

A Drowning

No cries or sighs
No tears or wailing
Can move it
It remains impervious
To the suffering
Of a torn heart
And keeps turning its waters
Forgetting that it holds prisoner
The child
That the mother waits for
On the shore.

Fleur de vie

Un frisson la frôle,
De fines perles glacées glissent
Le long des tempes brûlantes :
Le cœur se déchire,
Le corps se tend, s'affaisse.
Un vagissement cristallin
Envahit l'air
Fait se dérider.
L'heureuse néophyte
Se laisse engourdir,
Goûtant la satisfaction
D'une longue attente
Qui la sacre mère.

Berceuse noire

Chante
Chante ta meilleure complainte
A l'enfant
Frappé à mort
Qui s'endort à jamais
Berce
Berce-le tout doucement
Pour que son petit corps
Meurtri par les balles
Puisse connaître
Un léger soulagement
Avant de rejoindre
Nos Héros.

A Flower of Life

A shiver touches her
Delicate icy beads sliding
Along burning temples:
Her heart is pulled apart,
Her body tenses up, then sags back
A crystalline cry
Fills the air
Relaxing her face.
The blessed novice
Lets herself go slack
Tasting the satisfaction
Of a long wait
That consecrates her a mother.

Black Lullaby

Sing
Sing your best lament
For the children
Struck by death
And sleeping forever
Cradle
Cradle them gently, gently
That their tiny bodies
Bruised by bullets
Might know
A slight relief
Before they rejoin
Our Heroes.

A Thomas Sankara

Non
Tu n'as pas été un fou
Tu ne pouvais pas l'être
Puisque ton peuple
En pleurs
A couru
Vers ta tombe barbelée.

For Thomas Sankara

No
You were not a fool
You could not have been
Since all your people
In tears
Ran
Toward your barbed wire tomb.

A Um Nyobé Ruben

Ta mort sauve la victoire
   A ta source
Qui ne viendra désormais boire !

Ta vie de privations
Ta vie de tentations
S'étale à mes yeux
Et m'invite à suivre
A travers les sentiers épineux
Tes pas calmes et silencieux.

Apprends-nous à lutter dans l'espérance
Apprends-nous à donner sans défaillance
Apprends-nous à reconnaître sous tout don suspect
La piste glissante aux lendemains mauvais
Apprends-nous à savoir que dans une âme pure
La vie, à peu d'exceptions, est une expérience dure
Apprends-nous dans l'émulation
A servir sans délation
Pour que nous t'apportions demain
   Pour bouquet
Le pays pour lequel tu mourus.

JEANNE NGO MAI (CAMEROON)

Born in 1933 in Ngambe, Cameroon, Ngo Mai earned a bachelor's degree from the University of Yaoundé in 1954. She pursued medical studies in France at Toulouse and received a doctorate in pharmacology. She lives in Yaoundé, where she works as a pharmacist.

For Um Nyobé Ruben

Your death preserves victory
    From now on
Who would not come to drink at your spring!

Your life of privation
Your life of temptation
Unfolds before my eyes
And invites me to follow
Down the thorny paths
Your serene and silent footsteps

Teach us to struggle with hope
Teach us to give without weakness
Teach us to recognize beneath any suspect gift
The slippery track to evil tomorrows
Teach us to know that for a pure heart
Life is with few exceptions hard experience
Teach us in our emulation
To serve without incrimination
That we may offer you, tomorrow
    As a bouquet
The land for which you died.

Désespoir

La mère s'est assise,
A côté du petit malade
Son père de l'autre côté,
Sa sœur aux pieds,
Son frère à la tête,
Mais le corps du petit enfant
A continué d'être secoué de râles.

Sa mère lui a tenu la main,
Son père lui a posé sur la tempe
La paume de sa main,
Sa sœur lui a caressé doucement
Tout doucement le pied,
Son frère lui a parlé doucement
Tout doucement à l'oreille,
Mais le corps du petit enfant
A continué d'être secoué de râles.
Pendant que son père l'absorbait
De son regard muet
Sa sœur l'a tenu plus fort
Son frère a murmuré
        "Il ne peut pas me laisser jouer seul"
Les larmes doucement,
Tout doucement ont coulé des yeux
De sa mère.
Mais les yeux du petit enfant se sont
Peu à peu fermés.
Alors la mère a déchiré l'air
D'un cri perçant.

Despair

The mother sat down
Beside the sick child
His father on the other side
His sister at his feet,
His brother at his head,
But the body of the little child
Continued shaking with rasping coughs

His mother held his hand
His father placed on his temple
The palm of his hand,
His sister caressed softly
Very softly his feet
His brother spoke softly
Very softly in his ear
But the body of the little child
Continued shaking with rasping coughs
While his father held him
With his silent gaze
His sister hugged him more tightly
His brother whispered
    "He can't leave me to play alone"
The tears slowly
Very slowly fell from the eyes
of his mother.
But the eyes of the small child
little by little closed
And then the mother shattered the air
With a piercing scream.

Ce n'est pas ma faute . . .

Ce n'est pas ma faute
Si personne ne me comprend
Si j'ai
Pour m'exprimer
Un langage absurde

Les arbres aussi
    les vents
    les fleurs
    et les eaux
S'expriment à leur manière
Etrange pour les humains

Prenez-moi pour arbre
    pour vent
    pour fleur
    ou pour eau
Si vous voulez me comprendre.

CLÉMENTINE NZUJI
(DEMOCRATIC REPUBLIC OF CONGO)

Nzuji was born in 1944 in Tshofa, Zaire, and attended school in Kinshasa. She received a degree in African languages from the National University of Zaire in 1972 and a doctorate of humanities from the Sorbonne in 1983. She has written extensively on African languages, literature, and art and published a novel and short stories as well as poetry. She lives in Belgium, where she teaches at the Catholic University of Louvain.

It's not my fault . . .

> It's not my fault
> If no one understands me
> If I must
> Express myself in
> An absurd language
>
> The trees also
> > and the winds
> > the flowers
> > and the waters
> Express themselves in their own way
> Strange to human beings
>
> Take me as a tree
> > as wind
> > as flower
> > or as water
> If you want to understand me.

Kasala

Je suis une fille à la peau noire
                    fine et luisante
Je suis une négresse au grand cœur
                    Cœur d'eau fraîche
                    Cœur d'hirondelle en vol
                    Cœur souffrant et pleurant
                    Cœur timide d'un oiselet malade.

Je viens de ce pays étrange
                    qu'on ne peut définir
Ce pays étrange où l'homme
                    est l'être suprême de l'univers sensible
Ce pays où l'animé parle à l'inerte
                    et l'esprit à l'ombre
                    par le vent crépusculaire
Je viens du pays noir et lumineux
                    pays du soleil et des eaux.

Chez moi, les arbres parlent aux poètes
                    la brise aux amants
                    et l'ondée aux aimées
Chez moi, la harpe a existé
                    avant que David fût
Je suis du pays où les mains travaillent
                    et le cœur parle
Chez moi, les enfants ramassent le bois mort
                    pour en faire des feux
Je suis du pays où en haut soufflent les vents
                    et en bas résonne l'harmonie
Le pays où coule une eau toujours nouvelle
                    depuis nos ancêtres
                    et de générations en générations
Chez moi, l'aquilon apporte des sons d'au-delà
                    et les oiseaux des messages
Je viens du pays à quoi rien ne ressemble
                    le pays où l'ami se fait frère
                    et l'amie sœur
Le pays où l'art est avant toute chose . . .

Kasala

I am a girl with black skin
                    smooth and glistening
I am a Black woman with a big heart
                    Heart of fresh water
                    Heart of a swallow in flight
                    Heart of pain and tears
                    Timid heart of a sick little bird.

I come from this strange land
                    that no one can define
This strange land where humans
                    are supreme beings of the tangible universe
This land where the animate speak to the inert
                    and the spirit to the shadow
                    out of the twilight wind
I come from this black and luminous land
                    land of sun and waters.

In my country, trees talk to poets
                    the breeze to lovers
                    and the shower of rain to beloved women
In my country, the harp existed
                    before David did
I am from the land where hands work
                    and the heart speaks
In my country, children gather fallen wood
                    to light fires
I am from the land where the winds blow above
                    and harmony resonates below
Where new waters always flow
                    since the time of our ancestors
                    and from generation to generation
In my country the north wind carries the sounds of paradise
                    and birds carry messages
I come from a land that resembles no other
                    the land where a friend is a brother
                    or a sister
A land where art comes before everything . . .

Au mendiant

Au mendiant
Il faut donner des yeux
Pour qu'il voie la tête qu'il fait aux passants
Il faut donner des mains
Pour qu'il les tende aux bourgeois
Il faut donner une langue
Pour qu'il crie haut sa misère
Jusqu'à réveiller les corbeaux
Et à donner espoir aux hyènes
Qui attendent que refroidissent
Les yeux crevés
Les mains coupées
La langue arrachée du mendiant
Aux cimetières des ossements
Que sont nos places publiques.

Mon poème se veut délire

Mon poème se veut délire
Mon poème se veut folie
    délire de ceux qui souffrent
    folie de ceux qui ont perdu la joie.

Il se veut cicatrice
Il se veut vengeur
    Cicatrice de sublimes blessures
    Vengeur de cœurs écorchés.

Il se veut démence
Il se veut tourbillon
    Démence de ceux qui agonisent
    Tourbillon de ceux qui vont pleurer.

To the Beggar

To the beggar
You must give eyes
To see the face he offers passers-by
You must give hands
To hold out to the bourgeois
You must give a tongue
To shout his misery so loudly
That crows wake up
And hyenas regain hope
Awaiting
The punctured eyes
The severed hands
The torn-out tongue of the beggar turning cold
In the cemeteries of bone
Our town squares have become.

My poem wants to be delirium

My poem wants to be delirium
My poem wants to be madness
    delirium of those who suffer
    madness of those without joy.

It wants to be a scar
It wants to be an avenger
    A scar of sublime wounds
    An avenger of flayed hearts.

It wants to be dementia
It wants to be a whirlwind
    Dementia of those who are dying
    Whirlwind for those who will cry.

Dernier secret

la lumière s'est éteinte avec l'aurore
la houle a pris la place du premier matin
n'est-ce pas ta présence qui remue ma pensée
n'est-ce pas elle qui irrise ma vision
hélas !
la brume qui l'entoure m'empêche de le dire
mais le souvenir hors de toi n'a plus de sens
tu y nais et y grandis dès la première lueur

que n'ai-je refusé
le frôlement de tes doigts sur ma joue
la promenade de ta main sur la mienne
au moment de l'adieu

Variante

l'innocence s'est éteinte au petit matin
la chair a pris possession du dernier secret
n'est-ce pas ton appel qui remue ma pensée
n'est-ce pas elle qui excite mon émoi
. . .
la blessure qui m'habite m'empêche de le dire
même le départ, sur elle, n'a pas de prise
elle renaît et grandit dès la tombée du soir

que n'ai-je arrêté
la tricherie de tes doigts sur mon visage
la promenade de ta joue sur ma joue
au moment de l'au-revoir

Jubilation

j'ai éteint dans la nuit
la lumière du chevet
pour sentir à mes côtés
la chaleur de ta nudité.
illuminés de nos joies

Final Secret

light has died with the dawn
its wave has replaced the first morning
isn't it your presence that disturbs my thought
isn't it that rainbow in my vision
alas!
the surrounding haze keeps me from saying so
but memory without you is meaningless
there you were born and grew in the first gleam

why didn't I refuse
the light touch of your fingers on my cheek
the dance of your hand in mine
at the moment of farewell

Variant

innocence died in the early morning
flesh took possession of the final secret
isn't it your call that disturbs my thought
isn't it that which excites my feeling
. . .
the wound that dwells in me keeps me from saying so
even departure has no hold on it
it is reborn and grows at the fall of night

why didn't I stop
the cheating of your fingers on my face
the brushing of your cheek on my cheek
at the moment of good-bye

Exultation

in the night I turned off
the bedside lamp
to feel beside me
the warmth of your nakedness.
illumined by our joy

215   Clémentine Nzuji

les ténèbres de minuit
attendent pour jubiler
l'harmonie sublime des amants.
et tes doigts qui minaudent
dans le néant de la nuit
noire comme moi-même dévêtue
me parcourent de part en part
dans la quiétude et le frisson.

Sourire

ton sourire frôlait ma joue
comme une prière
prêtresse je n'osais happer
ton attente silencieuse

nous étions distants
et pourtant côte à côte
dans l'espace entre nos corps
couraient d'infinis secrets

Variante

ta lèvre effleurait mon cou
avec un murmure
craintive je n'osais toucher
les traces de sa brûlure

nous étions côte à côte
et pourtant lointains
le silence entre nos doigts
taisait d'infinis accords

the darkness of midnight
waits to exult
the sublime harmony of lovers.
and your fingers that smile
at the nothingness of the night
as black as me naked
go over me inch by inch
with calmness and passion.

Smile

your smile touched my cheek
like a prayer
priestess I did not dare seize
your silent hope

we were distant
and yet side by side
in the space between our bodies
infinite secrets passed

Variant

your lip brushed against my neck
with a whisper
timid I did not dare touch
the traces of its burning

we were side by side
and yet so far apart
the silence between our fingers
kept the infinite harmonies quiet

Solitude

Solitude mon amour !
Quelle histoire que la nôtre
Et que d'années elle dure !
Enfant déjà, tu étais avec moi,
Sur les cours d'écoles
Dans les rues de la ville.
Par la main doucement tu me prenais
Ensemble nous faisions de si longues promenades
Mes chagrins d'enfant tu les connais
Mes pleurs d'épouse tu les as partagés
Que de souvenirs mon tendre amour !
Lorsque mes mains cherchent dans la nuit,
C'est toi qu'elles étreignent
Lorsque je cherche des mots de réconfort
Doucement tu me les chuchotes
Que t'importe l'amour d'un homme ?
Pourquoi espérer une tendre caresse ?
Tes mains de soie me caressent
Ton amour généreux m'inonde
T'inquiète pas pour moi ma mère
Ne te fais pas de soucis pour mes vieux jours mon fils
Je suis liée pour la vie à un amour,
Un amour sans fin, un amour solitaire !

—*22 août 1998*

ANNETTE PEMBÉ (CAMEROON)

Pembé was born in 1961 at Kribi, Cameroon, and attended grammar schools there. She went to the University of Dakar for her undergraduate degree, then pursued media studies at the University of Yaoundé. She lives in Yaoundé, where she works for International Computer Systems.

Solitude

Solitude my love!
What a story is ours
And the years it's lasted!
As a child you were already with me,
In the school yards
In the streets of the city.
You gently held my hand
Together we took long walks
You know my childish heartbreaks
My tears of a wife, you shared
So many memories, my tender love!
When my hands reach in the night,
It is you they embrace
When I seek words of comfort
Gently you whisper them to me
What do I care about the love of a man?
Why hope for a tender caress?
Your hands of silk caress me
Your generous love surrounds me
Mother, don't worry about me
Son, don't agonize over my old days
I am tied to this love for life
An endless love, a solitary love!

Le macchabée

A chaque pas s'ajoutent d'autres
Depuis l'aube des temps il marche
Toujours il suit la même route.

Il a humé tous les vents
Il a bu à toutes les sources

Aux heures ont succédé les jours
aux jours des mois, aux mois des années.

Il hait les horloges, car elles limitent le temps.
Seule lui importe cette route, la sienne.

Il s'arrête de temps en temps.

Un jour il a connu l'extase de l'amour,
un autre il a même fait un enfant.

Mais il a continué sa route.

Sous le soleil, la lune et les étoiles,
sous la pluie, la mousson et l'harmattan.

Sur certaines rives on lui présentait des fruits,
mais lui, ne voulait que les fruits de la vie,
Qu'il cueillait et foulait si facilement sous ses pas.

Le bonheur pour lui était plus haut, plus loin.

Un jour sur la route il ramassa le miroir,
il y découvrit un inconnu.
Qui n'avait plus de dents car il avait croqué trop de fruits :
Les mûrs, les pas mûrs, et même les verts.

Qui n'avait plus de cheveux
tous étaient tombés sur la route.

Alors doucement sur le pavé il s'allongea,
il s'endormit d'un long sommeil,
Le seul qu'il ait jamais fait,
Depuis qu'il avait entamé sa marche vers l'infinitude.

The Living Dead

To each step he adds many more.
Since the dawning of time, he walks
Always, he follows the same path.

He breathed in every wind
He drank from every spring

Hours were followed by days
days by months, months by years.

He hates clocks, for they limit time.
Only this road, his own, matters to him.

He stops from time to time.

Once he came to know the ecstasy of love,
once he even fathered a child.

But he continued to follow his path.

Under the sun, the moon and the stars
in the rain, the monsoon and the harmattan.

On certain shores he was offered fruit,
but he only wanted the fruits of life,
that he picked and so easily trampled.

Happiness for him was on higher ground, further away.

One day on his path he picked up the mirror,
he discovered in it a stranger.
One who was now toothless from biting too many fruits:
The ripe, the unripe, even the green.

Who no longer had any hair
all of it fallen out along his way.

Then carefully he lay down on the roadside
to sleep a long sleep,
the only one he would ever sleep,
since he began his walk toward infinity.

Annette Pembé

Extraits de *Et . . . sens*

Entre l'instant du temps
et
Le temps que dure l'instant
surgit

KARITE

[...]

La malice coquine son visage calebasse
feutré de poussière
pigment de kola
Parée d'une aura prolifique
La grâce nonchalante de son beurre
parfume ses ports de senteurs cacaoyères

EVANESCENTE

[...]

Alors
le flot de ses yeux se fait calme
Karité hurle sa voix dans le silence oppressant
La communauté se resserre en majuscule

Dans un geste de survie
les monologues coulent
vers un trou sans fond

PASCALE QUAO-GAUDENS (CÔTE D'IVOIRE)

Quao-Gaudens was born in 1963 in Côte d'Ivoire and educated there through secondary school. She moved to Paris in 1986 and worked as a book illustrator and in a small publishing house. She returned to Abidjan in 1994 and started her own book business, working with local publishers and distributors across the region.

From *Et . . . sens*

Between the moment of time
and
The time a moment lasts
Suddenly

SHEA

[. . .]

The tease flirts with her calabash face
layered in dust
pigment of kola
adorned in a prolific aura
the nonchalant grace of her butter
perfumes her home with fragrant cocoa beans

EVANESCENT

[. . .]

Then
The flood in her eyes becomes calm
Shea wails her voice in the oppressive silence
The community tightens into capital letters

As an act of survival
the monologues flow
towards an endless void

Les incantations rattachent chaque individu
à lui-même
attachent l'existence
au pilier de nos vies
en minuscule

Karité se mêle au prologue de la mort
dans cette pièce blanche aromatisée d'éther
où sur un lit veille l'histoire d'un être qui erre

[…]

Les mots taquinent ses sens
Le verbe rampe dans ses antres
Elle désire
se répandre
entendre
la voix
de son chant

Et la musique s'écrie :

Rythme !
Ton corps Karité
D'un balancement
Pour vibrer en sourde insolence

Cambre tes courbes dans un rituel
Envoûte ses refuges

Entend ma cadence

[…]

D'ailleurs
dans chaque foyer
aux envers des murs
de pierre d'argile de béton
LES ENFANTS DU PARADIS
hurlent des silences et des oublis

The incantations connect each individual
                    to themselves
            join their existence
                        to the pillar of our lives
                    in small letters

Shea mingles with the prologue to death
in this white room scented with ether
where on a bed a story keeps watch over someone who wanders

[…]

The words taunt her senses
The verb creeps into her lair
        She desires
                    to be scattered
                    to hear
                        the voice
                            of her song

And the music cries:

Rhythm!
Shea your body
Balanced
To vibrate in a deaf insolence

Arch your curves into a ritual
Bewitch his refuge

Understand my rhythm

[…]

Besides
in each home
on the wrong side of the walls
of stone of clay of concrete
THE CHILDREN OF PARADISE
            wail of silences and oblivions

Des ténèbres éblouissent leurs regards primesautiers
Jets d'instants du désespoir
                    engendré par la folie d'un soir
                    lugubre d'ironie
Synthèse de nos écarts charnels
Cris inassouvis des ricanements ancestraux
        se blottissant dans nos oeufs
                    Heu !

                    eux...
    qui gloussent de nous avoir à jamais reproduits
                    Trahis d'un nous-même sublime
                    Déchus de nos corps mal imbriqués
                    par manque de symbiose
                            de projets

Nés d'un ailleurs mal informé
        d'un instant à jamais moment
            Moment d'oubli

Out of darkness their impetuous gaze dazzles
Flashing instants of despair
                            born of a night's madness
                            dismayed by irony
Synthesis of our carnal deviations
Unappeased cries of sneering ancestors
    Crouched in our eggs
                            Zzz!
                                        they . . .
    who cluck at having bred us
                            Betrayed by our sublime selves
                            Fallen from our distorted bodies
                            by lack of symbiosis
                                    of design

Born of an ill-informed elsewhere
    of an instant forever moment
        Moment of oblivion

World Music

Elle chante
elle déchante
la world musique
d'ailleurs et de partout,
universelle dans son approche.

Elle brasse,
elle embrasse,
la world musique
un continent blanc qui court
pour attraper la culture plurielle

Elle mélange,
elle métisse,
la world musique,
les rythmes traditionnels de partout
à grands renforts d'électronique.

Elle se vend,
elle se prostitue
la world musique
en sauce douteuse et mièvre
d'une culture qui se marketise.

FATOUMATA SIDIBÉ (MALI)

Born in 1963 in Bamako, Sidibé attended the Catholic University in Louvain, Belgium, where she studied economics and then took a degree in journalism. She currently works as a journalist, editor, and translator in Brussels, and is president of the Belgium committee Ni Putes Ni Soumises. Her recent novel is Une saison africaine, *published in 2006.*

World Music

> World music
> sings
> and unsings
> world music
> from elsewhere and from everywhere,
> its approach is universal.
>
> World music kisses,
> it stirs up
> the white continent running
> to capture the plural culture
>
> World music
> mixes up,
> it crossbreeds
> the traditional rhythms of everywhere
> with electronic reinforcement
>
> It sells
> it's prostituted
> world music
> the dubious and insipid soup
> of a culture for sale.

Mon fils

La lune veille
et l'enfant sommeille
Sa tête sort de la couverture
comme une fleur qui sourit à la vie
Son souffle est comme une mélodie nocturne
Sa bouche comme un bouton de rose.
Mon fils endormi
et moi debout dans le grand silence.
O corps qui fut mien !
O chair de ma chair !
Ma gloire d'être mère éclate,
jaillit de la source de mon cœur
comme des myriades d'étoiles
sabrant le ciel.
Il y a longtemps
tu voguais dans mon ventre
comme un voilier sur une mer calme.
En te faisant naître,
Je me suis donné la vie.

My Son

The moon keeps watch
and the child sleeps.
His head emerges from the covers
like a flower smiling at life.
His breath is like a nocturnal melody
His mouth like a rosebud
My son asleep
and I standing in complete silence.
Oh body that once was mine!
Oh flesh of my flesh!
My glory in being a mother bursts
Rising from the bottom of my heart
like a myriad of stars
shooting across the sky.
Long ago
you sailed in my womb
like a boat on a calm sea.
In giving birth to you
I gave life to myself.

Vivre sa jeunesse sans être discourtois

Vivre sa jeunesse sans être discourtois,
Vivre sa jeunesse sans être narquois,
Vivre sa jeunesse sans se prostituer,
Vivre sa jeunesse sans s'intoxiquer.

Jeunesse rime avec gentillesse.
Jeunesse rime avec politesse.
Jeunesse rime avec liesse.

Vivre sa jeunesse en bonne santé,
Dans la gaîté,
Dans le labeur,
Dans l'espoir,
Dans la réflexion.

Jeunesse ne rime
Ni avec beuverie,
Ni avec toxicomanie
Ni avec abîme.

La jeunesse,
Ce cadeau du ciel sans égal
Chérissez-la !

FATOUMATA SANO SISSOKO (GUINEA)

Sissoko was born in 1954 in Dakar, where she received her early education and then earned a degree from the University Cheikh Anta Diop. She completed further degrees in public administration, Latin American studies, and Spanish, and currently teaches French at a secondary school in Conakry, Guinea. She also founded and now administers a kindergarten in Conakry.

Live your youth without being unkind

Live your youth without being unkind,
Live your youth without cunning,
Live your youth without prostituting it,
Live your youth without drunkenness.

Youth rhymes with kindness.
Youth rhymes with good manners.
Youth rhymes with joy.

Live your youth in health,
In joy,
In work,
In hope,
In reflection.

Youth doesn't rhyme
With debauchery,
Nor with addiction
Nor with despair.

Being young,
This unequaled blessing of heaven
Cherish it!

Mon jouet préféré

Ma poupée d'hier est devenue réelle
Elle est aussi vivante que moi
Joli bébé respirant la santé
Ta tranquillité m'inquiète
Tes pleurs m'attristent
Tes rires me soulagent
Mon jouet préféré
Ta joie me préoccupe
J'aime quand tes pieds rament l'air rempli d'allégresse
Le mouvement de tes petites mains roses rend ton bain
    euphorique
Ton nez minuscule symbolise ton innocence
Tu es tout doux quand tu dors les poings fermés
Ton corps tout entier est la vie en miniature.

FATOU SONKO (SENEGAL)

Sonko's work appeared in Anthologie de la jeune poésie sénégalaise *(1999), an anthology of poems selected from among open submissions by young Senegalese writers. Neither the editors of that anthology nor those of this present anthology have been able to contact her or discover any further biographical information.*

My Favorite Toy

My doll of yesterday is now real
She is as alive as I am
Pretty baby breathing health
Your tranquility disquiets me
Your tears sadden me
Your laughter relieves me
My favorite toy
Your joy engrosses me
I love when your feet row through the joyful air
The moving of your small rose hands turns your bath
    ecstatic
Your miniscule nose represents your innocence
You are all gentleness when you sleep with your fists closed
Your whole body is life in miniature.

La clé

Enfant, mon espoir,
Tout dans la nature
Te parle :
Le soleil, la lune
L'oiseau qui passe
Le fleuve qui coule
Et même la pierre froide
Si tu sais
Ecouter, regarder, et sentir,
Tu trouveras la clé de l'univers.

Le tam-tam

Connais-tu le langage du tam-tam ?
Le tam-tam du jour de fête,
Le tam-tam qui appelle les génies,
Le tam-tam du lutteur ruisselant de sueur,
Le tam-tam de la mort.
Connais-tu le langage du tam-tam ?
C'est le secret de la forêt.

FATOU NDIAYE SOW (SENEGAL)

Sow was born in 1956 in Tivaouane, Senegal. She attended local schools and then the Teachers Training College in Rufisque. She worked as a teacher in Dakar, but traveled widely (Europe, Canada, the United States) for writers festivals and the promotion of children's literature, and it is for her children's poetry that she is best known. She died in 2004.

The Key

> Child, my hope,
> Everything in nature
> Speaks to you:
> The sun, the moon
> The bird that flies
> The river that flows
> And even the cold stone
> If you know how
> To listen, to look, and to feel
> You will find the key to the universe.

The Drum

> Do you know the language of the drum?
> The drum of the day of celebration,
> The drum that calls the spirits,
> The drum of the wrestler dripping with sweat
> The drum of death
> Do you know the language of the drum?
> It's the secret of the forest.

Berceuse

Eye Sama Néné Touty !
Si tu sèches tes larmes
Je te ferai un berceau
Des merveilles de l'Univers
Eye Sama Néné
Si tu sèches tes larmes
Je te porterai dans un pagne
Tissé de rayons de soleil
Eye Sama Néné
Si tu sèches tes larmes
Je t'offrirai un bouquet d'étoiles
Pour retrouver ton sourire aurore
Eye Sama Néné !
Ayo Béyo Béyo
Ayo . . .

Un jour, à Gorée

Sais-tu mon fils
que sur ces mers profondes
ont vogué un jour les lourds négriers
Emportant à jamais
Les pionniers au verbe fertile.
Sur la vague bleue
Ils ont parsemé l'espoir.
Et là-bas au delà des frontières
Quand les "blues" remuent
Les entrailles de la nuit,
c'est ton frère qui te rappelle
Le pacte de sang.

Lullaby

Ey Sama Neene Tutti!*
If you dry your tears
I will sing you a song
Of the wonders of the Universe
Ey Sama Neene
If you dry your tears
I will carry you in a pagne
Woven out of sun rays
Ey Sama Neene
If you dry your tears
I will give you a bouquet of stars
To find again your smile at dawn
Ey Sama Neene!
Aayoo Béyo Béyo
Aayoo . . .

*"Hush my little baby" Eye or ayo is an interjection meant to
soothe; sama means my; neene means baby; tutti means little,
small.—EDITOR'S NOTE

A Day on Gorée

Do you know my son
On these deep seas
Heavy slaveships once sailed
Taking away forever
The pioneers with fertile tongues
On the blue wave
They scattered hope
And over there, way beyond the borders
When the "blues" shake
The guts of the night
That's your brother ~ reminding you of
The blood pact.

Au seuil du néant

Dans ce monde vampire,
Me voilà remplie de mon exil.
Laissez-moi redécouvrir
Le Baobab Originel
Où dort l'Aïeul
Dans la rumeur profonde
De sa solitude première.
Laissez mon œil éclaté
De myriades de soleils,
Voyager dans l'espace-temps sans rivages
Et dissoudre dans la foi les râles de l'angoisse,
Et pêcher des éclats d'espoir
Dans l'horizon pourpre du couchant
Pour ennoblir le rapace humain
Bourreau ou victime
A la recherche d'une étoile lointaine
Lointaine
Cachée aux portes du silence.
Dans l'Univers de l'espérance
Laissez-moi déchiffrer
Au pied du Baobab Originel
Le message de mes cauris,
Où je lis
Que chaque époque vit son drame
Chaque peuple ses souffrances
Mais qu'aux portes du Néant
Chacun S'ARRÊTE et PENSE.

On the Threshold of Nothingness

In this vampire world,
Here I am filled with my exile.
Let me rediscover
The Original Baobab
Where the Ancestor sleeps
In the deep murmur
Of his original solitude.
Let my eyes gleam
With a myriad of suns,
Voyaging across time and space without shores
And dissolving into faith the cries of anguish
And fishing for glimmers of hope
In the purple horizon of dusk
To ennoble rapacious humanity
Executioner or victim
In search of a distant star
Distant
Hidden behind doors of silence
Inside the Universe of hope
Let me decipher
At the foot of the Original Baobab
The message of my cowrie shells
Where I read
That every epoch lives its drama
Every people their suffering
But that before the doors of Nothingness
Each one PAUSES and THINKS.

Extraits de *Latérite*

IL EST DES CRIS PUISSANTS
OÙ PERCE LA MISÈRE
ET DES FEMMES VOILÉES
OÙ SE TAISENT LES REFRAINS
IL EST AUSSI
DES POINGS FERMÉS
OÙ BATTENT
LES VIOLENCES
COMME UN HOMME ENCHAÎNÉ
À SA PROPRE SOUFFRANCE.

[...]

RACONTE-MOI
LA PAROLE DU GRIOT
QUI CHANTE L'AFRIQUE
DES TEMPS IMMÉMORIAUX
IL DIT
CES ROIS PATIENTS
SUR LES CIMES DU SILENCE
ET LA BEAUTÉ DES VIEUX
AUX SOURIRES FANÉS
MON PASSÉ REVENU
DU FOND DE MA MÉMOIRE

VÉRONIQUE TADJO (CÔTE D'IVOIRE)

*Born in 1955 in Paris of an Ivorian father and a French mother,
Tadjo was raised in Abidjan, Côte d'Ivoire. She received an
undergraduate degree from the University of Côte d'Ivoire and a
doctorate in Anglo-American studies from the Sorbonne. Besides
poetry Tadjo has written an impressive number of children's books
that she also illustrates. She has published several novels, including*
L'ombre d'Imana, *which was a product of the FestAfrica project
to memorialize the Rwandan genocide. One of the most widely
published contemporary francophone authors, she currently lives in
South Africa.*

From *Latérite*

THERE ARE POWERFUL CRIES
WHERE MISERY PIERCES
AND VEILED WOMEN
WHERE REFRAINS GO UNSUNG
THERE ARE ALSO
CLENCHED FISTS
WHERE VIOLENCE
BATTERS
LIKE A MAN CHAINED
TO HIS OWN SUFFERING

[…]

TELL ME
THE WORD OF THE GRIOT
WHO SINGS THE AFRICA
OF TIME IMMEMORIAL
HE SPEAKS
OF THOSE ENDURING KINGS
ON THE PEAKS OF SILENCE
AND THE BEAUTY OF ELDERS
WITH THEIR WITHERED SMILES
OF MY PAST RETURNED
FROM THE DEPTH OF MY MEMORY

COMME UN SERPENT TOTEM
À MES CHEVILLES LIÉ
MA SOLITUDE
ET MES ESPOIRS BRISÉS
QU'APPORTERAIS-JE
À MES ENFANTS
SI J'AI PERDU LEUR ÂME ?

[...]

IL Y A LONGTEMPS DÉJÀ
QUE J'AIME CHANTER TES PAS
ET ÉCOUTER TON SOUFFLE
AU MILIEU DE LA NUIT
IL Y LONGTEMPS QUE TON ODEUR
POSSÈDE TOUS MES SENS
ET QUE TA VOIX RÉSONNE
DE MILLE ÉCHOS LOINTAINS
LONGTEMPS QUE TON SOURIRE
ESQUISSE MES PENSÉES
ET QUE TES DOIGTS AGILES
TISSENT MES JOURNÉES
BIEN LONGTEMPS QUE JE SAIS
LE RYTHME DE TON POULS
ET LE VELOURS NOIR
DE TA PEAU OMBRAGÉE.

[...]

TU VERRAS
JE SUIS UNE SORCIÈRE
SI TU ÉCOUTES MA PAROLE
TES DENTS POUSSERONT
EN RANGÉES DOUBLES
ET TA GORGE
ROUCOULERA
DE RIRES EN CASCADE.

[...]

LIKE A SERPENT TOTEM
COILED AROUND THE ANKLES
OF MY SOLITUDE
AND SHATTERED HOPES . . .
WHAT WILL I BRING
TO MY CHILDREN
IF I HAVE LOST THEIR SOUL?

[. . .]

FOR A LONG TIME NOW
I'VE LOVED SINGING TO YOUR STEPS
AND LISTENING TO YOUR BREATH
IN THE MIDDLE OF THE NIGHT
FOR A LONG TIME NOW YOUR SCENT
HAS POSSESSED MY SENSES
AND YOUR VOICE RESONATED
WITH A THOUSAND DISTANT ECHOS
FOR A LONG TIME YOUR SMILE
HAS SKETCHED MY THOUGHTS
AND YOUR AGILE FINGERS
HAVE WOVEN MY DAYS
FOR A LONG LONG TIME NOW I HAVE KNOWN
THE BEAT OF YOUR PULSE
AND THE BLACK VELVET OF YOUR
SHADED SKIN

[. . .]

YOU WILL SEE
I AM A WITCH
IF YOU LISTEN TO MY WORDS
YOUR TEETH WILL GROW
IN DOUBLE ROWS
AND YOUR THROAT
WILL GURGLE
WITH CASCADING LAUGHTER

[. . .]

LA VIE EST FAITE
DE RONCES ET D'ÉPINES NOIRES
JE L'AURAIS VOULUE
PLUS MÛRE ET MOINS AMÈRE
MAIS TU SAIS
LA LIMITE DES CHOSES
RECULE À CHAQUE INSTANT
LES VISAGES SE CHANGENT
ET LES AMOURS S'ÉCRASENT
LES UNS CONTRE LES AUTRES
TU LE SAIS BIEN
AU SOIR DE TA FRAYEUR
IL NE RESTE QUE TOI.

Amitié

L'amitié
Est précieuse
Garde-la
Protège-la
Tu en auras besoin
Ne la jette pas
Ne la casse pas
Ne la néglige pas
Garde-la
Dans un coin
De ton coeur
Si tu veux
Dans un coin
De tes pensées
Si tu veux
Mais garde-la
Car l'amitié
N'a pas de frontière
Et ses limites
Sont celles du monde
Elle a les couleurs
De l'arc-en-ciel
Et la beauté

LIFE IS MADE
OF THISTLES AND DARK THORNS
I WOULD HAVE WISHED IT
MORE RIPE AND LESS BITTER
BUT YOU KNOW
THE LIMITS OF THINGS
PUSH BACK AT EACH MOMENT
FACES ARE CHANGED
AND LOVES ARE CRUSHED
EACH AGAINST THE OTHER
YOU KNOW VERY WELL
IN THE NIGHT OF YOUR TERROR
NO ONE REMAINS BUT YOU

Friendship

Friendship
Is precious
Guard it
Protect it
You will need it
Don't throw it away
Don't break it
Don't neglect it
Guard it
In a corner
Of your heart
If you want
In a corner
Of your thoughts
If you want
But guard it
Because friendship
Has no boundary
And its limits
Are those of the world
It has the colors
Of the rainbow
And the beauty

247   **Véronique Tadjo**

Du rêve
N'écoute jamais
Ceux qui disent
Qu'elle n'existe plus
Elle est là
Elle est à toi
Quand tu veux
Il suffit
D'ouvrir
les yeux.

Crocodile

Ce n'est pas facile d'être un crocodile
Surtout si on n'a pas envie
D'être un crocodile
Celui que vous voyez
Sur la page opposée
N'est pas bien
Dans sa peau
De croco
Il aurait aimé
Etre différent
Il aurait aimé
Attirer
Les enfants
Jouer
Avec eux
Converser
Avec les parents
Se balader
Dans
Le village
Mais, mais, mais

Quand il sort
De l'eau

Of a dream
Don't even listen to
Those who say
It no long exists
It is there
It is yours
Whenever you want
You just
Open
Your eyes.

Crocodile

It's not easy to be a crocodile
Especially if you don't want
To be a crocodile
The one you see
On the opposite page*
Is not happy
In his croc's
Skin
He would have liked
To be different
He would have liked
To attract
Children
Play
With them
Talk
With their parents
Walk around
In
The village
But, but, but

When he comes out
Of the water

Les pêcheurs
Lancent des sagaies
Les gamins
Détalent
Les jeunes filles
Abandonnent leurs canaris

Sa vie
Est une vie
De solitude
Et de tristesse

Sans ami
Sans caresse
Nulle part
Où aller

Partout
Etranger

Un crocodile
Crocodile
Végétarien
Et bon à rien
Qui a
Une sainte horreur
Du sang

S'il vous plaît
Ecrivez
Ecrivez à :
Gentil Crocodile
Baie N° 3
Fleuve Niger

Fishermen
Throw spears
Children
Take off
Young girls
Abandon their water jugs

His life
Is a life
Of solitude
And sadness

Without a friend
Without affection
Nowhere
To go

Everywhere
Stranger

A Crocodile
Vegetarian
Crocodile
And good for nothing
Who has
A holy horror
Of blood

Please
Write
Write to:
Nice Crocodile
Bay No. 3
Niger River

In the original publication of this poem, Tadjo's drawing of a crocodile appeared on the opposite page.

Extraits de *A mi-chemin*

Partir / revenir
ces allées et venues
de la vie
nous laissent fatigués
lassés que rien ne brise
l'exigence du temps

[...]

Il te fait l'amour
et pourtant
tu n'oses pas
le toucher
son corps
comme un tam-tam
de guerre
Il te fait l'amour
et pourtant tu ne sais pas
quoi penser

[...]

Il faut apprendre
à se séparer
connaître les mécanismes
qui aident à s'éloigner
sans briser les liens
sans casser les sentiments
Il faut apprendre
à se quitter
sans se perdre

[...]

La racine des pierres
plonge très loin dans l'oubli
Elle se gave des mémoires
que la terre rejette

[...]

From *Midway*

Leaving/Returning
these goings and comings
of life
leave us worn out
weary that nothing can shatter
the exigency of time

[…]

He makes love to you
and yet
You do not dare
touch him
his body
like a war
drum
He makes love to you
and yet you do not know
what to think

[…]

One has to learn
how to part
to know the mechanisms
that help to break away
without breaking ties
without destroying feelings
one has to learn
to leave
without being lost

[…]

The root of stones
plunges deep into oblivion
It is crowded with memories
that the earth rejects

[…]

Les portes de la ville sont closes
Nous mourons
d'une lente suffocation

On nous a menti
On nous a vidé les entrailles
mangé la tête
volé l'espoir

Dans cette ville
qui hurle
ses inégalités
Dans cette ville
désabusée
où tout se perd
l'amitié / l'amour
le silence / le souvenir

Où l'enfance se gaspille
Court les rues
pour quelques pièces
et fouiller les ordures
Où l'enfance se gaspille
déambule
au fil des jours
au fil des heures
de son errance

Tant de lendemains salis
Tant d'oublis inutiles
Tant de destins saccagés

Nous irons chercher l'espoir
et nous le sortirons
de son enclave profonde

Refusant
l'indifférence
et l'abandon

Nous irons chercher
l'espoir.

The doors of the city are closed
We are dying
from a slow suffocation

They have lied to us
They emptied our bowels
devoured our head
stole our hope

In this city
that howls
its inequalities
In this city
disabused
where all is lost
friendship/love
silence/memory

Where childhood is squandered
Running the streets
for a few coins
and rummaging the garbage
Where childhood is squandered
drifting
day by day
on the thread of the hours
wandering

So many tomorrows dirtied
So much forgotten uselessly
So many destinies wasted

We will go in search of hope
and we will pull it out
of its deep enclave

Refusing
indifference
and abandonment

We will go in search of
Hope

Elle dit qu'elle marchait dans la ville

Elle dit qu'elle marchait dans la ville et qu'alors, elle a senti des contractions fortes et rapprochées. Elle s'est pliée en deux en se tenant le ventre.
Elle dit qu'elle sentait quelque chose de chaud couler le long de ses jambes et qu'avant d'arriver à l'hôpital, elle était toute trempée. Elle dit que le sol était taché de rouge et qu'elle avait perdu son enfant.

[…]

Hier, neuf hommes ligotés contre des poteaux. A onze heures, le tir a commencé.

Première rafale : tout était fini. Mais l'un d'entre eux a relevé la tête.

Deuxième rafale : il n'était toujours pas mort.

Troisième rafale : sa tête s'est affalée sur sa poitrine.

[…]

Dans un aéroport, un petit garçon est tué à coups de mitraillette. Dans un aéroport, des corps criblés de balles attendent les ambulances.
Des valises éventrées, une odeur de poudre, de sang et de peur pèse sur le silence.
Commando terroriste. Attentat reconnu. La mort au hasard.

[…]

Il n'y a qu'une seule histoire d'amour que nous habillons et déshabillons avec nos mots et nos espoirs, une seule vraie saison du cœur où l'univers peut éclore, un seul moment de grâce pour renaître et reconstruire le monde envers et contre tout.

She says she was walking around the city

She says she was walking around the city and suddenly she felt strong contractions, close together. She doubled over holding her stomach.
She says she felt something warm running down her thighs and before reaching the hospital she was completely soaked. She says the ground was stained red and she had lost her baby.

[…]

Yesterday. Nine men tied to stakes. At eleven o'clock, the shooting began.

First volley: it was finished. But one of them lifted his head.

Second volley: He was still not dead.

Third volley: his head flopped onto his chest.

[…]

Inside an airport, a little boy is killed by machine gun.
Inside an airport, the bodies riddled with bullets wait for ambulances.
Smashed suitcases, the smell of gun powder, of blood and fear weigh on the silence.
Terrorist commando. Attack accounted for. Random death.

[…]

There is only one story of love that we dress and undress with our words and our hopes, a single true season of the heart when the universe comes alive, a single moment of grace for rebirth and for remaking the world come hell or high water.

Soirée à Mbélélane

Quand la lune suit ses caprices
Quand les étoiles dorment
Quand le ciel porte son manteau de deuil
Alors sur la chaude Afrique
Les portes des cases se referment sur leurs mystères
Ah ! Que luise la lune !
Que scintillent les étoiles
Pour que Mangoné le conteur
Invite le Roi de la jungle
La Déesse du fleuve
Le Roi, la Reine et les courtisans
Du royaume de Mbélélane
Qui insuffleront à nos petites âmes
Toutes les valeurs de l'Afrique.

OUMY BAALA THIONGANE (SENEGAL)

Thiongane's work appeared in Anthologie de la jeune poésie
sénégalaise *(1999), an anthology of poems selected from among
open submissions by young Senegalese writers. Neither the editors
of that anthology nor those of this present anthology have been able
to contact her or discover any further biographical information.*

Evening at Mbelelane

When the moon follows its whims
When the stars sleep
When the sky wears its coat of mourning
Then across the warmth of Africa
The doors of huts close on their mysteries
Ah! May the moon shine!
May the stars gleam
So that Mangone the story teller
May invite the King of the jungle
The Goddess of the river
The King, the Queen, the courtiers
Of the kingdom of Mbelelane
They will breathe into our young souls
All of Africa's ideals.

Je voudrais être griot

Je voudrais être griot,
Pour faire danser les mots,
Les moduler sur ma langue,
Et les faire glisser sur mes lèvres;
Les reprendre dans l'air,
Pour les refondre, les éclater,
Les polir, les caresser et les faire voler.

Je voudrais être griot, et d'une voix forte
Rompre le silence de la nuit,
Marteler les consciences endormies,
Secouer les voiles obscurcissants,
Créer une fissure
Qui laisse passer la lumière,
Et maintenir les yeux éveillés.

Je ne voudrais être griot,
Ni du Roi, ni du Fort, ni du Riche,
D'aucune Puissance . . .

Je voudrais être griot,
Pour ne m'intéresser
Qu'à ce qui construit l'homme.

ORTHENSE TIENDRÉBÉOGO (BURKINA FASO)

*Born in Guinea, Tiendrébéogo was raised and received her
education in Burkina Faso, graduating from the University of
Ouagadougou in 1984. She worked as a comedienne and as a
singer and has written for the theater. After receiving an advanced
degree in letters from the University of Bourgogne, she returned to
Ouagadougou, where she currently lives, working as a permanent
lecturer at the university there. Besides her poetry Tiendrébéogo has
published critical essays and four volumes of short stories.*

I Would Like to Be a Griot

> I would like to be a griot,
> To make words dance,
> Modulate them on my tongue,
> And make them slip across my lips;
> Recapture them in the air,
> To melt them again, explode them,
> Polish them, caress them and make them soar.
>
> I would like to be a griot, and with a loud voice
> Smash the silence of the night,
> Hammer on the sleeping conscience,
> Shake off the obscuring veils,
> Open a fissure
> That would let the light escape
> And keep the eyes awake.
>
> I do not want to be the griot,
> Of the King, the Strong, the Rich,
> Nor of any Power . . .
>
> I would like to be a griot,
> To be involved
> Only in what fashions a human being.

Le village

Peut-on jamais oublier le village ?
Peut-on jamais oublier ses rives
d'où monte le soir le clapotis de l'eau ?

Peut-on jamais oublier ses sources ?
Peut-on jamais oublier ses feuilles de bananiers
qui bruissent dans les ténèbres ?
Ecoute ce chant qui passe :
c'est un chœur d'enfants dans la pirogue
qui glisse dans la rivière

Sens-tu vibrer l'air du jour
et sens-tu frémir la terre grasse
quand l'ardeur du train bouscule le silence des montagnes ?

Regarde le soleil qui s'endort
comme lui étale ta natte et dors
car demain est un autre jour.

MARIE-LÉONTINE TSIBINDA (CONGO)

Born in 1953 in the town of Girard, Republic of Congo, Tsibinda received a master's degree in English literature from the University of Brazzaville. She published her first poetry in 1978, and has since published several books of poems as well as a novella, Les pagnes mouillés, *which won the UNESCO-Aschbery prize in 1996. She has lived in Canada since 2001.*

The Village

Can you ever forget the village?
Can you ever forget its shore
from where the splashing of water rises in evening?

Can you ever forget its springs?
Can you ever forget its banana leaves
that rustle in the darkness?
Listen to the song that unfolds:
it is a chorus of children in the pirogue
that glides on the river

Can you feel the air of the day vibrate
and can you feel the rich soil tremble
when the fire of a train pushes through the silence of the
mountains?

Look at the sun falling asleep
like him unfold your mat and sleep
for tomorrow is another day.

Il chante un cœur

Il chante un chœur
dans mon cœur
indocile, ma main
détourne le bruit
des mots-fureur
qui bouillonnent en moi
et trace d'indéchiffrables arabesques
perdues sur les sentes
inviolables du destin.

Senteur sauvage

Ton haleine sur mon visage
c'est la mer sur le visage
qui va et qui revient
et qui revient, et qui revient

toi vers qui je viens
quand fleurit la nuit
toi vers qui mes pensées
s'allument quand s'éteint le soleil

toi nombril profond
triangle des bermudes
rivage, visage, paysage
sauvage des jours farouches

toi qui m'allume
me brûle, m'incendie
et me ramène vers le rivage
à la rencontre de nouveaux visages.

Singing a Heart

A chorus sings
in my heart
stubborn, my hand
diverts the noise
of the words of fury
boiling inside me
and traces indecipherable arabesques
lost on the inviolable paths
of destiny.

Wild Scent

Your breath on my face
is the sea on a face
the sea that goes and comes
and comes back and back again

toward you I come
when the night flowers
Toward you my thoughts
blaze when the sun dies

your deep navel
a Bermuda triangle
shore, face, wild
landscape of ferocious days

you who set me on fire
burn me, set me ablaze
and return me to the shore
where the faces I encounter are new.

Un enfant d'ailleurs

(A Bonnie et K. Lee Brown)

Je ne veux pas que le temps
    efface à jamais
      ma mémoire

Je ne veux pas que le soleil
    calcine à jamais
      mes semences

Je ne veux pas que la pluie
    emporte à jamais
      mes petites chansons

toi enfant
d'Afrique
d'Amérique
d'Asie
d'Europe
de l'Océanie
tends-moi la main
fais sonner ton rire
fais chanter ton cœur
viens, vivons un rêve
un rêve fantastique
qui aura pour anneau
tous les cris d'oiseaux
de toutes les forêts du monde.

A Child of Elsewhere

(for Bonnie and K. Lee Brown)

I do not want time
    to erase forever
    my memory

I do not want the sun
    to scorch forever
    my seeds

I do not want the rain
    to wash away forever
    my little songs

you child
of Africa
of America
of Asia
of Europe
of Oceania
give me your hand
make your laughter ring
make your heart sing
come, let's live a dream
a fantastic dream
like a ring to be made
of all the bird cries
of all the forests in the world.

Le sang encore le sang

Les sirènes hurlent
les hiboux ululent

rien ne va plus

raccourcis ton pagne
femme
rase ta tête
homme
accroche-toi à ta mère
enfant.

Le séisme approche
la terre frémit déjà
mais très bientôt
elle tremblera craquera
engloutira sans repos

le sang encore le sang
rouge comme le feu
inondera la terre

combien de bougies perdues ?
combien de fosses communes
creusées depuis ?
combien de têtes portées disparues?

Le sang encore le sang
chaud comme le feu
rouge comme le soleil
inondera la terre.

Blood and More Blood

Sirens howl
owls ululate

nothing is fine anymore

lift up your pagne
woman
shave your head
man
cling to your mother
child.

The earthquake is coming
the earth is already shaking
but very soon
it will shake and split
engulf without stopping

blood and more blood
red like fire
will cover the earth

how many lost candles?
how many mass graves
dug since then?
how many heads declared missing?

Blood and more blood
hot like fire
red like the sun
it will engulf the earth.

Au pays du silence

Il paraît qu'au pays du silence
ceux qui font le gros dos
un nigaud leur saigne le dos
pour en faire un gigot.

Comme une lumiére

Femme des eaux
je te salue
que ne sècherai-je pas la mer
pour retrouver la trace
de tes sœurs parties
vers une destinée inconnue
sans nos bénédictions
sans nous dire adieu
vers des saisons nouvelles

Femme des eaux
quel enfant portes-tu
celui du lac Kounkouati
du lac Numbi
ou encore celui des eaux profondes
du lac Bleu

Femme des eaux
femme de Poulou
femme des eaux
femme du Kongo
je te salue

Je te salue
pour le serment de fidélité
jamais prêté et que tu portes
comme une lumière

In the Land of Silence

They say that in the land of silence
when someone has a big head
a fool bleeds their head
and turns it into a leg of mutton.

Like a Light

Woman of the waters
I salute you
what sea would I not empty
to recover the trace
of your sisters long gone
toward an unknown destiny
without our blessings
without their good-byes
toward new seasons

Woman of the waters
which child do you carry
the one of Kounkouati Lake
of Numbi Lake
or of the deep waters
of Blue Lake

Woman of the waters
woman of the Poulou
woman of the waters
woman of the Kongo
I salute you

I salute you
for the oath of fidelity
never taken and still carried
like a light

Femme des eaux
femme des forêts
quelles légendes n'inventerai-je pas
pour que tes dents éclairent la nuit
et que l'enfant ronronnant à ton sein
ne kwashiorkore plus

Femme des eaux
femme-soleil
femme des vents
femme-sœur
femme-mére
femme-amie
femme-amante
femme-fétiche
femme-épouse
femme-sirène
je te hisse plus
haut que la tour des tours
Femme des eaux
je te salue
toi image de paix d'amour et de douleur.

Woman of the waters
woman of the forests
what legends would I not invent
to see your teeth illuminate the night
and make sure that the child purring at your breast
does not kwashiorkor* any longer

Woman of the waters
sun-woman
woman of the winds
sister-woman
mother-woman
friend-woman
lover-woman
fetish-woman
wife-woman
mermaid-woman
I raise you higher
than the tower of towers
Woman of the waters
I salute you
you the image of peace of love and of pain.

*Children's disease of malnutrition caused by starvation. It is
usually a noun, believed to derive from a Ghanaian language.
Here, the author, in an atypical usage, transforms the noun into a
verb.—EDITOR'S NOTE

Taka

Un rang de perles de cristal tchèques ou slovaques
Un rang de perles de cristal comme un chapelet
Un rang de perles de cristal pour le Sultan
Lorsqu'il récitera la sourate de l'Amour
Mon rang de perles de cristal entre les doigts

Une famille

Ma tête dans les mains du Sultan
Mes lèvres dans la bouche du Sultan
Le corps du Sultan dans mon corps
Le sang du Sultan dans mon corps
Mon corps sur le lit
Le lit dans la chambre
La chambre dans la Paix
La Paix devant l'océan
L'océan sans l'enfant
L'enfant sans la vie
Ma tête dans les mains du Sultan
Mes lèvres dans la bouche du Sultan
Le Sultan dans ma vie

SHAÏDA ZAROUMEY (NIGER)

Born in Bamako, Zaroumey lived until age ten in Niger, and she was educated in Niger, Mali, and France. She has traveled widely in Europe, Asia, and the Americas, working as a civil administrator for various African nongovernmental organizations.

Taka

A waist band of crystal beads, Czech or Slovak
A strand of crystal beads like prayer beads
A strand of crystal beads for the Sultan
When he recites the sura of Love
My strand of crystal beads between his fingers

A Family

My head in the Sultan's hands
My lips in the Sultan's mouth
The Sultan's body in my body
The Sultan's blood in my body
My body on the bed
The bed in the room
The room enclosing Peace
The Peace facing the ocean
The ocean without child
The child without life
My head in the Sultan's hands
My lips in the Sultan's mouth
The Sultan in my life

Le Sultan sous ma peau

Sous ma peau de fille triste
S'est glissé le Sultan
Le Sultan des sables d'or et d'argent
Des sables d'or et d'argent de notre Pays

The Sultan Under My Skin

Under my sad girl's skin
The Sultan slipped in
The Sultan of gold and silver sands
The sands, gold and silver, of our land

BIBLIOGRAPHY

Poetry

Abomo-Maurin, Marie-Rose. *Minkul mi nlem: Epine de mon espoir.* Yaoundé, Cameroon: Editions de la Ronde, Collection bleue, 2006.

Agbo, Berthe-Evelyne. *Emois de femmes.* Dakar, Senegal: Nouvelles Editions Africaines du Sénégal, 1999.

Agbo, Rufine. "Déception." In d'Almeida, ed., *Femmes africaines en poésie,* 25.

Aguessy, Dominique. *L'aube chante à plusieurs voix.* Namur, Belgium: Editions de l'Alcanthe, 1999.

———. *Comme un souffle fragile.* Paris: Editions Parole et Silence, 2005.

———. *Le gué des hivernages.* Paris: Editions La Porte, 2002.

Akplogan, Barbara. *Les mots d'amour.* Cotonou, Benin: Les éditions du flamboyant, 2003.

Alio, Salma Khalil. *Passion de la pensée.* Paris: Editions Le Manuscrit, 2004.

Amoi, Assamala. *Murmures de saisons.* Brazzaville, The Republic of Congo: Assamala Amoi, 2005.

———. *Poèmes de la rive du fleuve.* Brazzaville, The Republic of Congo: Editions Lemba, 2004.

———. "La vie." In d'Almeida, ed., *Femmes africaines en poésie,* 28.

Anaté, Kouméalo. *L'écrit du silence.* Marseille, France: Editions Les Belles Pages, 2006.

Aplogan, Edwige Araba. "L'aveugle et l'enfant" and "Demain l'Afrique, L'Afrique demain." In d'Almeida, ed., *Femmes africaines en poésie,* 25.

———. "Bleu" and "En attendant Brel, Dépestre, Parker, William, Aziz et les autres." Special issue on Benin, *Revue noire: Art comtemporain Africain* (Sept.–Oct. 1995): 24, 73.

Athié, Aminata. "Marchand de femmes." In Granel, Lemine, and Voisset, eds., *Guide de littérature mauritanienne,* 52–54.

Bassolé-Ouédraogo, Angèle. *Avec tes mots.* Ottawa, Canada: Editions Malaïka, 2003.

———. *Burkina Blues.* Quebec: Humanitas, 2000.

———. *Sahéliennes.* Ottawa, Canada: Editions L'Interligne, 2006.

Belibi, Virginie. *Vers enivrants.* Yaoundé, Cameroon: CLE, 1987.

Benga, Sokhna. *La ronde des secrets perdus*. Dakar, Senegal: Editions Maguilen, 2003.

Bénissan, Thécla G. "Voyage." In d'Almeida, ed., *Femmes africaines en poésie*, 30–31.

Boni, Tanella. *Chaque jour l'espérance*. Paris: L'Harmattan, 2002.

———. *Gorée île baobab*. Limoges, France: Editions le bruit des autres and Trois-Rivières; Canada: Editions Ecrits des forges, 2004.

———. *Grains de sable*. Limoges, France: Editions le bruit des autres, 1993.

———. *Il n'y a pas de parole heureuse*. Solignac, France: Editions le bruit des autres, 1997.

———. *Labyrinthe*. Paris: Editions Akpagon, 1984.

———. *Ma peau est fenêtre d'avenir*. La Rochelle, France: LarochelliVre and Editions Rumeurs des Ages, 2004.

d'Almeida, Irène Assiba. "Afrique." In *Black Women's Writing: Crossing the Boundaries*, edited by Carole Boyce Davies, 52–54. Frankfurt: Matatu, 1989.

———. "Cendres refroidies." In *Moving Beyond Boundaries: International Dimensions of Black Women's Writing*, vol. 1, edited by Carole Boyce Davies and 'Molara Ogundipe-Leslie, 181. London: Pluto Press, 1995.

———. "Crab." In *Talking Drums: A Selection of Poems from Africa South of the Sahara*, edited by Véronique Tadjo, 23, 33. London: A & C Black Publishers, 2000.

———. "Quicksand" and "Why Yallah Takes." In *New Poets of West Africa*, edited by Tijan Sallah, 106–8. Lagos, Nigeria: Malthouse Press, 1995.

———. "Sister, You Cannot Think a Baby Out!" In Chipasula and Chipasula, eds., *The Heinemann Book of African Women's Poetry*, 41–42.

———. "Le toucher du regard" and "L'enfant près du rivage." In d'Almeida, ed., *Femmes africaines en poésie*, 26–28.

———. "Treibsand." (German translation of "Quicksand.") In *Antilopenmond: Liebesgedichte aus Afrika*, edited by Peter Ripken and V. Tadjo, 114. Wuppertal, Germany: Peter Hammer Verlag, 2002.

———. "Vagues de plaisir," "Exorcisme," and "Atlantique des milles traversées." In "Flammes et reflets" (unpublished manuscript), 16, 63, 66–67.

Dao, Bernadette. *Poésie*. Ouagadougou, Burkina Faso: Imprimerie Presses Africaines, 1986.

———. *Poésie pour enfants*. Ouagadougou, Burkina Faso: Imprimerie Presses Africaines, 1986.

———. *Quote-part*. Ouagadougou, Burkina Faso: Imprimerie Nouvelle du Centre, 1992.

———. *Symphonie* (Soie et Soleil). Ouagadougou, Burkina Faso: Imprimerie Nouvelle du Centre, 1992.

Dati, Marie Claire. *Les caillots de vie*. Yaoundé, Cameroon: Presses Universitaires de Yaoundé, 2001.

———. *Les écarlates.* Yaoundé, Cameroon: Editions SOPECAM, 1992.

de Lallé, Madeleine [Madeleine de Lallé Kabore]. *Arc en vole.* Abidjan, Côte d'Ivoire: Edilis, 2006.

———. *Héritage.* Ouagadougou, Burkina Faso: Editions Sankofa, 2005.

Dembélé, Oumou. "L'Union." In d'Almeida, ed., *Femmes africaines en poésie,* 39.

d'Erneville, Annette M'Baye. *Chansons pour laïty.* Dakar, Senegal: NEA, 1976.

———. *Kaddu.* Dakar, Senegal/Abidjan, Côte d'Ivoire: Imprimerie A. Diop, 1966. (First published in 1965 as *Poèmes africains.*)

———. *Poèmes africains.* Paris: Centre d'art français (Prix des poètes sénégalais de langue française), 1965.

Diagne, Fatou Binetou. "Prière pour l'amour parfait," "Heurts et misères," and "Si tel était ton plaisir." In *Anthologie de la jeune poésie sénégalaise,* 13, 15.

Diakhate, Ndèye Coumba MBengue. *Filles du soleil.* Dakar, Senegal: NEA, 1980.

Diallo, Koumanthio Zeinab. *Comme les pétales du crépuscule.* Lomé, Togo: La Semeuse, 1994.

———. *Pellun Gonghi* (Poetry in Pular). Conakry, Guinea: Editions Ganndal, 1996.

———. *Pour les oiseaux du ciel et de la terre* (Poèmes pour l'enfance). Conakry, Guinea: Editions UNICEF, 1997.

———. *Les rires du silence.* Paris: L'Harmattan, 2005.

Diamonéka, Cécile-Ivelyse. *Voix des cascades.* Paris: Présence Africaine, 1982.

Diouf, Nafissatou Dia. *Primeurs.* Dakar, Senegal: Editions Le Nègre International, 2003.

Diouf, Ramatoulaye. "Femme." In *Anthologie de la jeune poésie sénégalaise,* 31.

Ewombe-Moundo, Elizabeth. *Le voyage abyssal.* Conakry, Guinea: Les Editions Gandal, 2002.

Faigou, Nafée Nelly. *Encres ancrées.* N'Djamena, Chad: Salon des belles lettres, 1997.

———. *Entre rêves et réalités.* N'Djamena, Chad: RLP, 1997.

———. *Taches d'instants égratignés.* N.p.: 1995.

Fall, Kiné Kirima. *Chants de la rivière fraîche.* Dakar, Senegal: NEA, 1975.

———. *Les élans de grâce.* Yaoundé, Cameroon: Editions CLE, 1979.

Fiadjoe Prince-Agbojan, Jémima. *Lumières sonores au coeur du silence.* Lomé, Togo: NEA/TOGO, 1992.

Houéto, Colette S. *L'aube sur les cactus.* Cotonou, Benin: Presses de l'I.N.F.R.E, 1981.

Ilboudo, Monique. "Fermée pour l'inventaire" and "Les Jupes." In d'Almeida, ed., *Femmes africaines en poésie,* 46–47.

Kam, Sophie Heidi. "Ecrire," "Sérénité," "Résolutions," and "Trouble." In Diop, ed., *Saison d'amour et de colère,* 27–28, 29, 30, 31.

Kanzié, Sandra Pierrette. *Les tombes qui pleurent.* Ouagadougou, Burkina Faso: Imprimerie Nouvelle du Centre, 1987.

Kimbekete, Lea. *Regard perdu*. Brazzaville, The Republic of Congo: Editions Lemba, 2006.

——. *Arc en ciel*. Abidjan, Côte d'Ivoire: Edilis, 2006.

Léllèl, Mallai. "Castration" (unpublished manuscript).

——. "Femme," "Miroir brisé," and "Obéissance." In *Encres* (Revue culturelle). Hors série (June 1996): 14, 15, 16.

——. "Linceul." In *Encres* (Revue du Club de la Promotion de la littérature et de la culture), 4 (Jan. 1996): 15.

——. "Sourire." In d'Almeida, ed., *Femmes africaines en poésie*, 48–49.

Liking, Werewere. *L'amour-cent-vies*. Paris: Publisud, 1989.

——. "Drôles de poésie" (unpublished manuscript). Performance in song, USA Tour, Fall 2003.

——. *Elle sera de jaspe et de corail* (Journal d'une misovire). Chant roman. Paris: L'Harmattan, 1983.

——. *"It Shall Be of Jasper and Coral" and "Love-across-a-Hundred-Lives."* Translated by Marjolijn de Jager. Introduction by Irène Assiba d'Almeida. Charlottesville: University Press of Virginia, 2000.

——. *On ne raisonne pas le venin*. Paris: Editions Saint-Germain-Des-Près, 1977.

——. *Orphée-Dafric*. In *Orphée-Dafric suivi de Orphée d'Afrique*. Paris: L'Harmattan, 1981.

Mare, Honorine. "Traces croisées," "Hélas," "Etranges compagnons," and "Le pays d'amour." In Diop, ed., *Saison d'amour et de colère*, 35, 36, 37, 38.

Mayaba, Hortense. "Quand la vie s'éteint" and "Le gros oeil du Bon Dieu." In d'Almeida, ed., *Femmes africaines en poésie*, 51.

Mba, Lucie. *Patrimoine II*. Paris: L'Harmattan, 2006.

Mbacké, Mame Seck. *Pluie-poésie les pieds sur la mer*. Paris: L'Harmattan, 2000.

Mvotto-Bina, Jeanne Irène. *Les fleurs du passé*. Yaoundé, Cameroon: Semences Africaines, 1977.

Ndiaye, Aminata. "J'irai à toi." In *Anthologie de la jeune poésie sénégalaise*, 34.

——. "Ndity," "Femme," and "Survie." In Diop, ed., *Saison d'amour et de colère*, 177, 178–79, 180–81.

Nébardoum, Derlémari Abdias. *Cri sonore*. Montreal: Editions d'Orphée, 1987.

Néné, Amélia. *Fleurs de vie*. Paris: Présence Africaine, 1980.

——. *Perles perdues*. Paris: Présence Africaine, 1998.

Ngo Mai, Jeanne. *Poèmes sauvages et lamentations*. Monaco: Les Cahiers Poètes de Notre Temps, 1967.

Ngom, Suzanne. "Est-ce donc normal?" and "Les oiseaux." In *Anthologie de la jeune poésie sénégalaise*, 20, 22.

Nzuji, Clémentine. *Gestes interrompus*. Lubumbashi, Democratic Republic of Congo: Editions Mandore, 1976.

——. *Impressions*. Kinshasa, Democratic Republic of Congo: Lettres Congolaises, O.N.R.D., 1968.

———. *Kasala.* Kinshasa, Democratic Republic of Congo: Editions Mandore, 1969.

———. *Lianes.* Lubumbashi, Democratic Republic of Congo: Editions Mandore, 1971.

———. *Murmures.* Kinshasa, Democratic Republic of Congo: Lettres Congolaises, O.N.R.D., 1968.

———. *Le temps des amants.* Kinshasa, Democratic Republic of Congo: Editions Mandore, 1969.

Pembé, Annette. "Macchabé." In d'Almeida, ed., *Femmes africaines en poésie,* 54–56.

———. "Solitude." In "Plume errante" (unpublished manuscript).

Quao-Gaudens, Pascale. *Et . . . Sens.* Paris: Publisud, 1988.

Sidibe, Fatoumata. "World Music" and "Mon fils." In d'Almeida, ed., *Femmes africaines en poésie,* 58.

Sissoko, Fatoumata Sano. "Vivre sa jeunesse sans être discourtois" and "Mon poisson rouge." In d'Almeida, ed., *Femmes africaines en poésie,* 58–59.

Sonko, Fatou. "Mon jouet préféré." In *Anthologie de la jeune poésie sénégalaise,* 26.

Sow, Fatou NDiaye. *Fleurs du Sahel.* Dakar, Senegal: NEAS, 1990.

———. *Takam-Takam "Devine, mon enfant."* Dakar, Senegal: NEA, 1981.

———. *Takam tiku: J'ai deviné.* Dakar, Senegal: NEA, 1988. 2nd ed. Cotonou: Les Editions du Flamboyant, 1993.

Tadjo, Véronique. *La chanson de la vie et autres histoires.* Paris: Editions Hatier, 1989.

———. *Latérite.* Paris: Hatier, 1984. Translated as *Red Earth* by Peter S. Thompson. Spokane: Eastern Washington University Press, 2006.

———. *A mi-chemin.* Paris: L'Harmattan, 2000.

Thiongane, Oumy Baala. "Soirée à Mbélélane." In *Anthologie de la jeune poésie sénégalaise,* 25.

Tiendrébéogo, Orthense Catherine. *Dix poèmes pour l'âge d'or* (Poésie pour enfants). Ouagadougou, Burkina Faso: Ministère de la Culture/Imprimerie Nationale du Burkina, 1994, 75–82.

———. "Je voudrais être griot." In d'Almeida, ed., *Femmes africaines en poésie,* 87.

Tsibinda, Marie-Léontine. *Demain un autre jour.* Paris: Editions Silex, 1987.

———. *Une lèvre naissant d'une autre.* Heidelberg, Germany: Editions Bantoues, 1984.

———. *L'oiseau sans arme* (Poésie pour enfants). Jouy-Le-Moutier, France: Bajag-Meri, 1999.

———. *Mayonbé.* Paris: Editions Saint-Germain-des-Près, 1980.

———. *Poèmes de la terre.* Brazzaville, Republic of Congo: Editions Littéraires Congolaises, 1980.

Zaroumey, Shaïda. *Alternances pour le sultan.* Niamey, Niger: Quantics, 1992.

Zirignon, Ida. *Au nom des pères, suivi de quelques aphorismes sur le nœuds de l'amour et de la haine.* Paris: L'Harmattan, 2005.

———. *Rwanda mon amour.* Cotonou, Benin: Editions du Flamboyant, 2001.

Anthologies and Critical Works on Poetry

Amoa, Urbain. *Poétique de la poésie des tambours.* Paris: L'Harmattan, 2002.

Anthologie de la jeune poésie sénégalaise. Paris: Editions Caractères, 1999.

Baadhio, Befer Hassane. *Hommage à la femme africaine: Poésie.* Ouagadougou, Burkina Faso: 1994.

Badaman, Maurice, Paul Ahizi, Joseph Amouma, and Daniel Zongo. *Portrait de siècles meurtris: Anthologie de la poésie de Côte d'Ivoire.* Ivry, France: Editions Nouvelles du Sud, 1993.

Bassolé-Ouédraogo, Angèle. "Sans pays! Langue, exil et self-identité diasporique." *Mots pluriels* 23 (March 2003). http://www.arts.uwa.edu.au/MotsPluriels/MP197index.html

Belvaude, Catherine. *Ouverture sur la littérature en Mauritanie: Tradition orale, écriture, témoignages.* Paris: L'Harmattan, 1989.

Boumgardt, Ursula, et Bonfour, Abdalah, eds. *Panorama des littératures africaines: Etats de lieux et perspectives.* Paris: L'Harmattan, 2000.

Bourdette-Danon, Marcel. *Les enfants des brasiers ou les cris de la poésie tchadienne.* Paris: L'Harmattan, 2000.

Boyd-Buggs, Debra. "Fleurs confisquées: L'écriture féminine au Niger." *Notre librairie* 118 (1994): 13–16.

Chemain, Arlette. "Ecriture féminine et transgression: Poésie du Congo." *Notre librairie* 118 (1994): 17–24.

Chevrier, Jacques, ed. *Anthologie africaine: Poésie.* Paris: Hatier, 1988.

———. *Anthologie africaine d'expression française. Volume II, la poésie.* Vanves, France: Hatier, 2002.

Chipasula, Stella, and Frank Chipasula. *The Heinemann Book of African Women's Poetry.* Oxford: Heinemann, 1995.

Collins, Georgina, ed. *The Other Half of History: An Anthology of Francophone African Women's Poetry.* Coventry, UK: Spon End, 2007.

Dakeyo, Paul, ed. *Anthologie de la poésie camerounaise.* Paris: Silex, 1982.

d'Almeida, Irène Assiba. "L'enfant au cœur des stratégies d'écriture des poétesses africaines." *Nottingham French Studies* 40, no. 1 (2001): 63–74.

———, ed. *Femmes africaines en poésie.* Bremen, Germany: Editions Palabres, 2001.

———. "'Le mot juste' de Tanella Boni, poétesse de Côte d'Ivoire." In *La revue des lettres modernes/Ecritures contemporaines,* 4 (2001): 141–54. Paris: Editions Minard.

Dia, Hamidou. *Poésie africaine et engagement: Parcours libre.* Paris: Acoria, 2003.

———, ed. *Poètes d'Afrique et des Antilles* (anthologie). Paris: Editions de La Table Ronde, 2002.

Diop, B. B., ed. *Saison d'amour et de colère: Poèmes et nouvelles du Sahel*. Dakar, Senegal: NEAS, 1998.

Diop, Samba. *Epopées africaines: Ndiadiane Ndiaye et El Hadj Omar Tall*. Paris: L'Harmattan, 2004.

Durand, Jean-François. *L'écriture et le sacré: Senghor, Césaire, Glissant, Chamoiseau*. Montpellier, France: Université Paul-Valéry III, 2002.

Epanga Yondo, Elolongué. *Kamerun! Kamerun! Poésie*. Paris: Présence Africaine, 1999.

Fonkoua, Romuald. "Roman et poésie d'Afrique francophone: De l'exil et des mots pour le dire." *Revue de la littérature comparée* 67, no. 1/265 (1993): 25–41.

Gey, Anne-Marie. *Anthologie de la poésie Négro-Africaine pour la jeunesse*. Dakar, Senegal: NEA/EDICEF, 1986.

Granel, Martin Nicolas, Idoumou Ould Mohamed Lamine, and Georges Voisset. *Guide de la littérature mauritanienne: Une anthologie méthodique*. Paris: L'Harmattan, 1992.

Herzberger-Fofana, Pierrette. "Annette Mbaye D'Erneville." In *Littérature féminine francophone d'Afrique Noire*. Paris: L'Harmattan, 2000.

Huannou, Adrien. *Anthologie de la littérature féminine d'Afrique Noire francophone*. Abidjan, Côte d'Ivoire: Les Editions Bognini, 1994.

Jasen, Jan. *Epopée, histoire, société: Le cas de Soundjata: Mali et Guinée*. Paris: Karthala, 2001.

Kabuta, Ngo Semzara. *Eloge de soi, éloge de l'autre*. New York: PIE-Peter Lang, 2003.

Labidi, Zineb. *Passagères*. Paris: Marsa éditions, 2000.

Larrier, Renée. "Les femmes poètes du Sénégal." *Présence francophone* 36 (1990): 45–56.

Luneau, René. *Chants des femmes du Mali*. Paris: Luneau Ascot Editeurs, 1981.

Mabelemadiko, N. N., ed. *Le Zaïre écrit: Anthologie de la poésie zaïroise de langue française*. Tübingen, Germany: H. Edmann Verlage, 1976.

Magnier, Bernard. *Poésie d'Afrique au sud du Sahara, 1945–1995*. Paris: Actes Sud/Editions Unesco, 1995.

Mamonsono, Léopold-Pindy, ed. *La Nouvelle génération de poètes congolais*. Brazzaville, The Republic of Congo: Editions Bantoues and Heidelberg: Kivouvou Verlag, 1984.

Mateso, Locha E., ed. *Anthologie de la poésie d'Afrique Noire d'expression française*. Paris: Hatier, 1987.

Maunick, Edouard J. *Poèmes et récits d'Afrique Noire, du Maghreb, de l'océan Indien et des Antilles*. Paris: Le Cherche midi éditeur, 1997.

Mbondé Mouangué, Auguste Léopold. *Pouvoirs et conflit dans Jèki la Njambé: Une épopée camerounaise*. Paris: L'Harmattan, 2005.

Mongo-Mboussa, Boniface. *Que peut la poésie aujourd'huit?* Paris: L'Harmattan, 2000.

Nkashama, Pius Ngandu, ed. *Littératures africaines: De 1930 à nos Jours.* Paris: Silex/ACCT, 1984.

Nkashama, Pius Ngandu, and Bernard Magnier. *L'Afrique noire en poésie.* Paris: Gallimard (Collection folio junior en poésie), 1986.

Pénel, J.-D., ed. *Anthologie de la poésie centrafricaine.* Paris: L'Harmattan, 1990.

Poésie des 1000 continents: Anthologie "paroles partagées." Dakar-Ponty, Senegal: Editions Feu de Brousse, 2005.

Poésie tchadienne d'expression française. N'Djamena, Chad: Editions ADELIT, 1994.

Ruelland, Suzanne, and Jean-Pierre Caprile. *Contes et récits du Tchad: La femme dans la littérature orale tchadienne.* Paris: Editions EDICEF, 1978.

Sall, Amadou Lamine. *"J'ai mangé tout le pays de la nuit,"* followed by *"Problématique d'une nouvelle poésie de langue française: Le long sommeil des Epigones."* Dakar, Senegal: NEAS, 1994.

Sall, Amadou Lamine, and José Muchnik, eds. *Le grain, le cœur et le mot.* Dakar-Ponty, Senegal: Les Editions de Brousse, 2001.

Sall, Babacar. *Poésie du Sénégal.* Paris: Editions Silex, 1988.

Sallah, Tidjan, ed. *New Poets of Africa.* Lagos, Nigeria: Malthouse Press, 1995.

Sène, Abdou, and Louis Camara, eds. *Tempête.* Dakar, Senegal: NEAS, 2000.

Tadjo, Véronique, ed. *Talking Drums: A Selection of Poems from Africa South of the Sahara.* London: A & C Black Publishers, 2000.

Tadjo, Véronique, and Peter Ripken, eds. *Antilopenmond: Liebesgedichte aus Afrika.* Wuppertal, Germany: Peter Hammer Verlag, 2002.

Tati-Loutard, J. B., and Philippe Makita, eds. *Nouvelle anthologie de la littérature congolaise d'expression française: Textes, 1977–2003, et histoire, 1953–2003.* Paris: Hatier, 2003.

Teulié, Gilles. *Afrique, musiques et cultures.* Montpellier, France: Université Paul-Valéry III, 2001.

Tompson, Peter. *Négritude et nouveaux mondes: Anthologie de la poésie noire africaine, antillaise, malgache.* Sandwich, Mass.: Wayside Publication, 1994.

COPYRIGHT ACKNOWLEDGMENTS

CARAF BOOKS

Caribbean and African Literature
Translated from French

Guillaume Oyônô-Mbia and
 Seydou Badian
Faces of African Independence:
 Three Plays
Translated by Clive Wake

Olympe Bhêly-Quénum
Snares without End
Translated by Dorothy S. Blair

Bertène Juminer
The Bastards
Translated by Keith Q. Warner

Tchicaya U Tam'Si
The Madman and the Medusa
Translated by Sonja Haussmann
 Smith and William Jay Smith

Alioum Fantouré
Tropical Circle
Translated by Dorothy S. Blair

Edouard Glissant
Caribbean Discourse: Selected Essays
Translated by J. Michael Dash

Daniel Maximin
Lone Sun
Translated by Nidra Poller

Aimé Césaire
Lyric and Dramatic Poetry, 1946–82
Translated by Clayton Eshleman
 and Annette Smith

René Depestre
The Festival of the Greasy Pole
Translated by Carrol F. Coates

Kateb Yacine
Nedjma
Translated by Richard Howard

Léopold Sédar Senghor
The Collected Poetry
Translated by Melvin Dixon

Maryse Condé
I, Tituba, Black Witch of Salem
Translated by Richard Philcox

Assia Djebar
Women of Algiers in Their Apartment
Translated by Marjolijn de Jager

Dany Bébel-Gisler
Leonora: The Buried Story of
 Guadeloupe
Translated by Andrea Leskes

Lilas Desquiron
Reflections of Loko Miwa
Translated by Robin Orr Bodkin

Jacques Stephen Alexis
General Sun, My Brother
Translated by Carrol F. Coates

Malika Mokeddem
Of Dreams and Assassins
Translated by K. Melissa Marcus

Werewere Liking
*"It Shall Be of Jasper and Coral" and
"Love-across-a-Hundred-Lives"*
Translated by Marjolijn de Jager

Ahmadou Kourouma
*Waiting for the Vote of the Wild
Animals*
Translated by Carrol F. Coates

Mongo Beti
The Story of the Madman
Translated by Elizabeth Darnel

Jacques Stephen Alexis
In the Flicker of an Eyelid
Translated by Carrol F. Coates and
Edwidge Danticat

Gisèle Pineau
Exile according to Julia
Translated by Betty Wilson

Mouloud Feraoun
*The Poor Man's Son: Menrad,
Kabyle Schoolteacher*
Translated by Lucy R. McNair

Abdourahman A. Waberi
The Land without Shadows
Translated by Jeanne Garane

Patrice Nganang
Dog Days: An Animal Chronicle
Translated by Amy Baram Reid

Ken Bugul
*The Abandoned Baobab:
The Autobiography of a
Senegalese Woman*
Translated by Marjolijn de Jager

Irène Assiba d'Almeida, Editor
*A Rain of Words: A Bilingual
Anthology of Women's Poetry
in Francophone Africa*
Translated by Janis A. Mayes